Differentiating
MATH
INSTRUCTION

Differentiating
MATH
INSTRUCTION

Strategies That Work for K–8 Classrooms!

William N. Bender

CORWIN PRESS
A SAGE Publications Company
Thousand Oaks, California

For information:

Corwin Press
A Sage Publications Company
2455 Teller Road
Thousand Oaks, California 91320
www.corwinpress.com

Sage Publications Ltd
1 Oliver's Yard
55 City Road
London EC1Y 1SP
United Stated

Sage Publications India Pvt. Ltd.
B-42, Panchsheel Enclave
Post Box 4109
New Delhi 110 017 India

Printed in the United States of America

Library of Congress Cataloging-in-Publication Data

Bender, William N.
Differentiating math instruction : strategies that work for K–8 classrooms! / William N. Bender.
   p. cm.
Includes bibliographical references and index.
ISBN 0-7619-3147-3 (acid-free paper : cloth) — ISBN 0-7619-3148-1 (acid-free paper : pbk.)
   1. Mathematics—Study and teaching. 2. Mathematics—Study and teaching (Early childhood) 3. Mathematics—Study and teaching (Primary) 4. Mathematics—Study and teaching (Elementary) 5. Individualized instruction. I. Title.
QA11.2.B46 2005
372.7—dc22

                                                                2004026604

This book is printed on acid-free paper.

05 06 07 08 09   10 9 8 7 6 5 4 3 2 1

Acquisitions Editor:	Robert D. Clouse
Editorial Assistant:	Jingle Vea
Production Editor:	Kristen Gibson
Copy Editor:	Kristin Bergstad
Typesetter:	C&M Digitals (P) Ltd.
Indexer:	Kay M. Dusheck
Proofreader:	Sally Scott
Cover Designer:	Rose Storey

Contents

Preface

HOW TO USE THIS BOOK

This book is intended for teachers who want additional ideas for differentiating instruction in the elementary math class. It is not intended as a text, but rather as a practical applications book.

I understand that teachers are very busy, and I wanted to develop a helpful book, filled with practical suggestions that can be immediately useful. Many of the simple tactics and instructional ideas here are forthright and may be immediately applied in almost any classroom. The instructional sections labeled "Teaching Tactics" and "Ideas From Teachers" represent immediately applicable ideas that should assist math teachers in grades from kindergarten through Grade 7 or 8. In particular, the "Ideas From Teachers" sections offer real-world differentiated instructional applications that teachers have suggested over recent years. If your time is limited, feel free to skip through the book in no particular order, looking at the sections that offer these helpful, easy to implement, practical tactics. Once you apply them, you'll find that your students' understanding and enjoyment of math skyrocket!

The good news is that you don't need to read the book cover to cover!

The "Teaching Tactics" describe instructional ideas in math that involve more complex instructional procedures than merely a new way to use music or movement to teach a simple math concept. These strategies represent the most effective way to differentiate within the math class and thereby meet the needs of all the students. These strategies are theory based, and enough information is provided for you to implement these strategies in your own class.

I have also provided "Web Site Reviews" in most chapters. Of course, these are not thorough critiques of these Web sites, nor does this brief list by any means exhaust the Web sites available to assist in mathematics instruction. Still, the use of these Web sites can greatly enhance your instructional efforts in math. Also, the links provided here will help you in your move toward a more differentiated math class.

Chapters 1 and 2 present the basics of differentiated instruction as applied in the math classes. Here you can learn what a differentiated math class looks like and how to establish a differentiated math lesson plan. The remaining chapters present instructional practices for a wide variety of specific areas in mathematics. Each of the chapters features the specific sections noted above, and each should provide you with some novel teaching ideas for differentiation in your classroom.

I sincerely hope this book assists you in your efforts to move toward differentiation in math, and I would be more than pleased to hear your thoughts on this book and/or your suggestions for additional instructional tactics that would help other teachers differentiate lessons in their math classes. Please feel free to e-mail me directly at wnbender@coe.uga.edu with your thoughts or teaching suggestions. While the volume of e-mails I receive often precludes an individual response, I do appreciate your thoughts, suggestions, and teaching tactics. I look forward to hearing from you!

Corwin Press gratefully acknowledges the contributions of the following people:

Daphne Alt
NBCT, Math Teacher
Andrews Middle School
Andrews, NC

John Woodward
Professor
University of Puget Sound
Tacoma, WA

Robert Cannon
NBCT, Math Teacher
La Paz Middle School
Salinas, CA

Pamela Goodner
NBCT, Math Teacher
Episcopal High School
Baton Rouge, LA

Mary Greaver
Math Teacher
Hillview Middle School
Palmdale, CA

Carlene Kirkpatrick
Math Teacher
North Oldham Middle School
Goshen, KY

About the Author

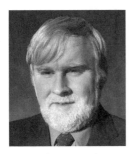

William N. Bender, Professor of Special Education at the University of Georgia, began his career by teaching eighth- and ninth-grade students in the public schools for several years prior to earning his PhD from the University of North Carolina in 1983. Since he has been in higher education, he has published more than 60 research articles and 11 books in special education and education. He specializes in instructional strategies and disciplinary strategies for all students, and particularly for students in general education classrooms who have disabilities such as learning disabilities, emotional disturbances, and attention disorders. He is recognized as a national leader in instructional tactics, as well as in distance education. His combination of practical strategies and easy humor leads to a demand for numerous workshops each year on various topics in education.

**CORWIN
PRESS**

The Corwin Press logo—a raven striding across an open book—represents the union of courage and learning. Corwin Press is committed to improving education for all learners by publishing books and other professional development resources for those serving the field of K–12 education. By providing practical, hands-on materials, Corwin Press continues to carry out the promise of its motto: **"Helping Educators Do Their Work Better."**

The Mathematical Brain

Differentiated Instruction and Mathematical Thinking

Strategies in this chapter include the following:

- Ten Brain-Compatible Teaching Guidelines for Math Instruction
- Ten Informal Tactics To Develop Number Sense
- Games and Activities for Developing Number Sense
- Ten Teaching Tactics for Providing Instruction in Math
- A Self-Evaluation Grid for Differentiated Instruction Lesson Planning

---

TEACHING MATHEMATICS THROUGH DIFFERENTIATING INSTRUCTION

Over the past two decades our nation has witnessed an emerging emphasis on mathematics instruction, and as a result achievement in math among students in the United States has been increasing (Harniss, Carnine, Silbert, & Dixon, 2002). In fact, within the past several years, math scores on several national indicators have increased (Strauss, 2003). However, there is still a considerable deficit between math scores of students in the United States and students in other modern nations of the world, and this deficit in math causes great concern among educators. The publication of the revised mathematical instructional standards by the National Council of Teachers of Mathematics (NCTM; 2000), the increased emphasis on national math standards in every state, and a seemingly endless series of reports that indicate many students do not achieve up to their potential in math, has placed mathematics instruction on the national agenda, second only to the

> Teaching tactics: Ten brain-compatible teaching guidelines for math instruction

emphasis on reading. Further, the emphasis on national math standards has received much research and media attention (Jitendra & Xin, 2002; Johnson, 2000). Research has shown that the vast majority of general education teachers—some 95%—are familiar with the NCTM standards and frequently address these standards in their teaching (Maccini & Gagnon, 2002).

The emphasis of instruction has changed somewhat, however, as a result of the revised NCTM standards. Students are expected to master a curriculum that has shifted away from computation, rote learning, and routine problem-practice activities toward an increased emphasis on reasoning, conceptual understanding, real-world problems, and connections between mathematical concepts (Johnson, 2000). Thus, much has changed in mathematics instruction, and teachers today must employ the most effective and efficient instructional methods possible for increasing cognitive involvement of all students with the math curriculum. Teachers are searching for instructional ideas that will assist in this regard.

The concept of differentiated instruction can be of great benefit to teachers in developing and designing their mathematics instruction for students with varying ability levels in the elementary education classroom. Moreover, the emphasis on brain-compatible instruction, one founding principle of differentiated instruction, can now inform teachers concerning what specific instructional tactics may be more useful (Bender, 2002; Tomlinson, 1999). While studies of how the human brain functions in reading tasks or math tasks have been undertaken for the past two decades, only recently has this emerging biomedical research—often referred to as brain-compatible research—progressed enough to inform teachers concerning effective instructional strategies for the math curriculum (Fuson & Wearne, 1997; Geller & Smith, 2002; Gersten, Chard, Baker, & Lee, 2002; Sousa, 2001). In particular, one aspect of the emerging research—multiple intelligences—seems to have struck a chord in the hearts and minds of educators within the past decade (Gardner, 1983, 1993). This perspective has provided one basis by which many math teachers have reformulated their instructional strategies. In fact, in several mathematics textbooks a multiple intelligences perspective is incorporated into the curriculum as well as in the teachers' instructor's manual!

This chapter will look at these two bases of differentiated instruction—multiple intelligences and brain-compatible instruction—with an emphasis in math instruction for students from kindergarten through Grade 8. First, the emerging research on brain-compatible instruction in math will be presented with a focus on practical classroom implications. Next, multiple intelligences will be presented as a viable basis for differentiating instruction in mathematics in order to accommodate the needs of all learners in the class. Finally, emphasis will be placed on the concrete, representational, abstract instructional construct common to math curricula today. This construct, though dated, can cross-fertilize the instructional suggestions from the more recent research areas, such as multiple intelligences, and provide the teacher with a new and interesting way to view all instruction in mathematics. In turn, this new sense of what mathematics instruction is will impact how teachers plan the instructional activities within the math curriculum.

Front

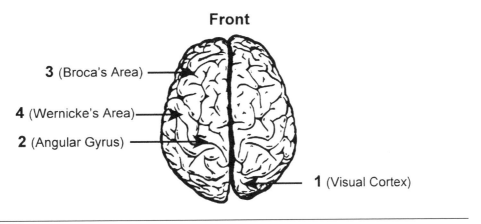

3 (Broca's Area)

4 (Wernicke's Area)

2 (Angular Gyrus)

1 (Visual Cortex)

Figure 1.1 The Brain

THE MATHEMATICAL BRAIN

Regions of the Mathematical Brain

Studies have demonstrated that, like most complex thought processes, there are a number of brain areas or different brain regions involved in mathematical processing (Sousa, 2001). The frontal lobe and parietal lobe of the cerebrum (i.e., the areas of the brain that are responsible for higher order thinking skills) are highly involved in mathematical understanding. The visual cortex is also involved, since students need to see most math problems, and the involvement of the visual cortex may be more complex than merely seeing the problem. Sousa (2001) suggested that the involvement of the visual cortex in almost all mathematical thinking indicates that math requires one to visualize math problems. Further, this would seem to be supported by studies over the years that have reported correlations between a child's mathematical ability and visualization capabilities (Grobecker & De Lisi, 2000; Jordan, Levine, & Huttenlocher, 1995).

Math is a highly complex skill that rests on many other brain functions as well. While reading is a complex skill that can be mastered relatively independently of other skills, math is not. Whereas a child does not need to learn math (or any other subject) in order to learn reading, the child does need to learn reading in order to master math, since so much of math involves reading either math problems or word problems. Even having students do a set of vertical or horizontal math facts problems requires the students to read the numerals within the problems (Barton, Heidema, & Jordan, 2002). Thus, reading is highly involved in most mathematical work in the public school classroom, and understanding the complex reading process may help show how complex math can be. Sousa (2001) presented a model of the "reading brain" that may be helpful here (see Figure 1.1).

As shown in Figure 1.1, four areas within the brain are primarily responsible for reading. First, the visual cortex takes in the stimulus of several squiggly lines on a page; for example:

$$6 + 3 = \underline{\hspace{1cm}}$$

Next, this stimulus is sent simultaneously to both the angular gyrus, which is the area of the brain that decodes sounds and processes written language, and to Wernicke's area—the area of the brain that is involved in comprehension of language. Next, Broca's area becomes involved; this brain area searches for meaning in the context of the numeral and its relation to other numerals presented in the problem. At this point, the frontal lobe and parietal lobe of the cerebrum become involved in "thinking through" the problem. These areas "imagine" the number problem and may even plan a strategy for solving it such as . . . "*Hold up six fingers, and count them, then hold up three more fingers and 'count on,' beginning with seven. Then say the answer.*"

> It takes some degree of "intentionality" on the part of the student to think through a math problem. Thus, another factor—motivation to learn—becomes critical. Students must be highly motivated to learn math because the learning process is so complex.

As this model demonstrates, mathematical thinking is a highly complex process that involves a number of areas within the human brain, including at a minimum the frontal lobe, the parietal lobe, the visual cortex, the angular gyrus, Wernicke's area, and Broca's area. Other areas beyond these may also be involved in the mechanics of thinking through math problems.

Thus, teachers must take the time to show the importance of mathematics in student's daily lives, in order for early learning to be successful. Motivation to learn math is discussed in more detail later, under "Priorities of the Emotional Brain."

Gender Maturation Within the Brain May Explain Early Achievement Differences

Research has recently examined how young boys and young girls experience math. Teachers have often noted that young girls mature a bit earlier than boys, particularly in areas such as linguistic skill and fine motor control. Of course, these are exactly the skills that early schooling depends upon for reading and writing, and when girls excelled in schools it was often assumed that girls simply matured faster overall. That concept is now being challenged. Brain research has documented that while young girls' brains do mature faster in these several areas, young boys seem to mature faster in certain other areas, including spatial and visual abilities. This may explain why young boys seem to do better in math than young girls (Strauss, 2003). At a minimum, it is not correct to assume that girls mature faster in all areas or in some overall way compared to young boys. Rather, the specific abilities associated with gender must be more carefully studied.

Hardwired Numbers in the Brain: One, Two, Three, Many . . .

A number of researchers have studied the normal maturation process of the developing brain in infancy and early childhood and have inquired about basic math skill. This research seems to suggest that only minimal math skills are hardwired into the brain during the normal maturation process (Geller & Smith, 2002; Sousa, 2001). These simple number recognition skills, like the development of language skills, would seem to be associated with normal maturation of the brain and central nervous system rather than schooling or preschool learning experiences.

In survival terms, this is quite understandable. Our ancestors' brains learned early in our evolutionary history to distinguish rapidly between one tiger that might be attacking and two tigers attacking in a coordinated attack plan, because the numbers and location of the tigers would suggest the best escape route or the best direction to run. Because movement was associated with survival, it also became somewhat hardwired in our brains—a point to which we will return later. Counting past the lowest numbers (i.e., numeration higher than 2 or 3), however, was not a selective survival skill, since that many tigers presumably left no viable escape route. Thus, the brain seems to be able to reflexively interpret the lowest numbers (i.e., 1, 2, and perhaps 3) and even to understand the numeration sequence of these numbers, but it cannot distinguish higher numbers without some instruction. Therefore, one way to understand the brain's response to observed objects in a set can be summed up in the phrase, *"One, two, three, many . . ."*

> **Essentially, the brain is hardwired for only minimal recognition of low numbers of objects, since certain minimal number- or set-recognition skills were associated with early survival skills. Thus, the lowest level of basic numeration seems to occur naturally.**

From the perspective of the math teacher, this means that instruction in math will be built almost entirely on prerequisite learned skills rather than on maturational-based knowledge. Thus, the importance of mastery of prerequisite skills prior to moving on to higher level skills cannot be overstated in the math curriculum from even the earliest levels on math instruction.

The Priorities of the Emotional Brain

Because of the research completed within the past 15 years, educators have realized that emotion and emotional intent play a much larger role in learning than previously thought (Bender, 2002; Sousa, 2001). For example, much of the information taken into the brain by the senses is first processed in the midbrain or the "emotional brain." Further, this emotional brain often serves as a filter through which stimuli must pass prior to being "considered" by the cerebrum (i.e., the forebrain and parietal lobe—or the "thinking" areas of the brain). Thus, a negative emotional response to a stimuli or particular type of task—such as a math problem—can in and of itself set up a lack of higher brain function involvement with the problem.

Of course, research has frequently shown that many students perceive math quite negatively or even fear math (Montague, 1997). In fact, such fears often provide a significant emotional barrier to mathematics achievement. For this reason, attending to a student's attitudes toward math and a student's motivation in learning math are critical. Teachers should both find ways to use "math-play" activities to make math less threatening, as well as scaffold students' work to assist students in their mathematics learning. Scaffolded instruction can offer support in mathematics that can, over time, offset the negative feelings many students have toward math.

IDEAS FROM TEACHERS

The "Right Answer, Different Question" Tactic

Every math teacher has had the experience of asking questions of students, calling on someone, and having the student give a wrong answer. This is often embarrassing for the student who answered the question wrong and may lead to negative emotional reactions to math. One option for reducing such potential embarrassment, involves the "Right answer, different question" tactic. When given a wrong answer by a student, teachers merely state, "There are no wrong answers, just answers to different questions." Here's an example.

Imagine instructing students on double-digit addition with regrouping, using the problem: 64 + 28.

Some excited student—a student who only last week learned double-digit addition without regrouping—may well answer "82!" Rather than immediately correcting him, the teacher could say something like, "I like that answer, but it really answers another question better. Let's figure out what question it answers. Who can help with that?"

At that point, rather than continuing with the problem above, the teacher should elicit answers from the class about how the problem above could be modified to result in an answer of 82. For example, one could change each digit in the ones place above, resulting in a problem of 61 + 21 = _____, or even 60 + 22 = _____. Teachers should stay with this line of discussion for a minute or so, having students generate several possible answers. To finish, the teacher should have the student who answered "82" come write his or her answer in the blank at the end of one of the new problems. That way, that answer is not wrong—it is just the answer to a different problem. Note that good instruction is taking place, even during the minute or so that the class is generating new problems. Further, this tactic reduces the negative emotions that are sometimes associated with math, and students become more inclined to participate in class questions. Note that once the teacher has finished the activity above, he or she should have the class return to the original problem.

BRAINS AS PRIORITIZING FILTERS

In the same fashion as the midbrain, or the "emotional brain," filters out information, many other brain areas function as filters, and any of these filters may prohibit learning in mathematics. When we consider the amazing number of stimuli to which our five senses are exposed every second, we can readily understand why the brain requires a variety of filtering mechanisms. Yet as teachers, we must make certain that the concepts we wish to teach get past the brain's filters that nature has provided.

There are several effective ways to do that. First, using novelty in teaching is critical. Tactics such as color coding or novel presentations of new information can greatly assist students in focusing on the mathematical content to be mastered. These tactics will assist every learner in mastering mathematics.

Perhaps more important is the teacher's presentation of the material. One brain function that allows the brain to filter information involves the brain's search for patterns, broad concepts, or organizing principles (Fuson & Wearne, 1997). Such broad concepts allow the brain to categorize and classify knowledge, and thus provide a type of "brain shorthand" by which concepts may be classified and mentally stored.

Many researchers are stressing instruction based on these "big ideas" or "essential questions" within the mathematics curriculum. These would include ideas such as the base-ten number system and concepts based on that system such as place value; expanded notation; commutative, associative, and distributive properties; and so on (see Harniss et al., 2002; Wiggins & McTighe, 1998). In order to get past the filtering function of children's brains, teachers should address, explicitly and repeatedly, the "big ideas" in each math unit. Further, teachers should assist students in making connections

> In effect, we, as teachers, can enhance the instruction we offer to all students if we highlight the "big ideas" or "organizing principles" within each individual math unit. Instruction that constantly highlights the big ideas would help the students' brains to organize the content.

between these big ideas across instructional units. With appropriate instruction based on these critical concepts, almost all learners can master the basic mathematics curriculum content in the elementary grades.

NUMBER SENSE

A number of researchers have begun to discuss the concept of "number sense" (Gersten & Chard, 1999; Griffin, Sarama, & Clements, 2003; Whitenack, Knipping, Loesing, Kim, & Beetsma, 2002). Number sense may be best understood as a student's conceptual understanding of basic number and numeration concepts such as counting, or recognizing how many objects are present in a set, and how a number may be used to represent that set of objects. The concept of number sense also involves recognizing that patterns make up the sequence of numbers. Gersten and Chard (1999) defined number sense as "fluidity and flexibility" with numbers.

> Number sense allows children to make sense of what the numbers mean, and children use number sense to make comparisons in the real world.

For example, students with number sense can translate real-world quantities and the mathematical world of numbers and numerical expressions (Gersten & Chard, 1999). These students are often quite capable of expressing the numbers in several different ways. They can show eight fingers by holding up five on one hand and three on the other, or when asked to show the same number another way, they can hold up four on one hand and four on the other. Students with number sense know that five objects are more than two objects; they recognize the relative size of the numbers though they may not know the actual difference between the two numbers.

In contrast, younger students without number sense may be able to count and recognize the figure that symbolizes the number (Gersten & Chard, 1999). They may be able to write or point to the numeral "5," but they do not comprehend the actual meaning of the number. They cannot yet tell if seven is more than five. While many children can count, children without number sense do not seem to have the concept of what the numbers mean or of the fact that numbers may be used to represent objects in a set. These problems may stem from a lack of understanding of one-to-one correspondence or simply from lacking the insight that higher numbers represent more "things" in a set. For older children, deficits in number sense would stem from the types of problems noted above. For example, students in the middle grades should realize that both ⅔ and ⅝ are larger numbers than ½, because of the numerator/denominator relationship (e.g., when the numerator is larger than half the value of the denominator or it is almost as large as the denominator, the fraction is more than ½). Without such recognition, students in the middle grades will show deficits in their understanding of fractions.

Initially, a child's early concept of number sense is acquired through informal interactions with the child's family prior to the school years. Unfortunately, if a child has not acquired number sense prior to kindergarten, the typical curriculum in school will not usually help him or her catch up (Gersten & Chard, 1999). Further, children raised in low socioeconomic environments tend to have less knowledge of number sense than students raised in middle to high socioeconomic homes (Gersten & Chard, 1999), because children from lower socioeconomic backgrounds have less of a chance to "double," "add," "subtract," and so on (Gersten & Chard, 1999).

Gersten and Chard (1999) suggest that number sense is critical to early education in math, and children without number sense will be at a great disadvantage. Further, number sense is necessary, but not sufficient, for problem-solving skills. Children must learn number sense in order to interpret mathematical problems in the real world, but they must also learn simple operations in order to begin mastery of problem solving. With this growing importance associated with number sense, it is unfortunate that few math curricula provide instructional tasks that address this critical phase in mathematics achievement. For this reason a series of instructional activities that will enhance students' number sense is provided later in this chapter.

MULTIPLE INTELLIGENCES: AVENUES FOR LEARNING MATH

The work of Howard Gardner, PhD, in multiple intelligences (Gardner, 1983, 1993) has had a profound influence on how mathematics is taught across the nation (Hearne & Stone, 1995; Katz, Mirenda, & Auerbach, 2002). As one example, Tomlinson's critically important construct of the differentiated classroom is based, in part, on the work of Dr. Gardner (Bender, 2002; Tomlinson, 1999). Dr. Gardner, in 1983, proposed that intelligence should be conceptualized as a variety of relatively discrete and independent intelligences rather than one overall measure of cognitive ability. He has now identified eight intelligences that represent different ways a child may understand or demonstrate his or her knowledge (Gardner, 1993). These include the following:

Linguistic: One's ability to use and manipulate language

Bodily/Kinesthetic: One's sense of one's body in space, and one's ability to move one's body through space

Logical/Mathematical: One's ability to understand logical propositions; one's "number sense"

Musical: One's ability to understand the structure of music as well as the rhythms, patterns that make up music

Spatial: One's ability to interpret spatial relationships, or to cognitively manipulate spatial relationships

Interpersonal: One's ability and skill at influencing others, reading subtle facial or bodily cues, and getting along with others

Intrapersonal: One's sense of self, including awareness of one's self and satisfaction with one's self overall

Naturalistic: One's ability to perceive relationships in the natural environment, to perceive categorical distinctions and various classifications, as well as the relationships between the classifications

While there is still considerable discussion of what these intelligences constitute, or even if other additional intelligences exist, the fundamental thrust of this work has been the effort to develop a wider array of instructional activities that offer learning options for each of these intelligences (Bender, 2002: Hearne & Stone, 1995). The proponents of multiple intelligences research encourage teachers to view these intelligences as avenues to learning or opportunities for learning. Students, in turn, are viewed as having various strengths and weaknesses, and the effective teacher must implement lessons that provide learning activities that address a wide variety of these intelligences in order to provide the best opportunity to learn for students who may have different strengths in particular intelligences. Teachers are encouraged to specifically plan their lesson activities with these intelligences in mind. Thus, over the course of a unit involving math facts content, a teacher would endeavor to have some activities that involved different intelligences.

TEACHING TACTICS

SAMPLE TIPS FOR TEACHING USING MULTIPLE INTELLIGENCES

Musical Intelligence Examples

1. Chanting of math facts is a good activity, and using rhythmic activities can greatly assist learning. Using the rhythm, "We will, we will rock you" and changing the addition facts (repeat that chant "One, two, three, rest" or "slap, slap, clap, rest" rhythm twice per fact and saying "one plus one is two; one plus two is three," and so on).

2. Other great tunes used by many teachers are the theme song from the old television show "The Addams Family" and "Row, Row, Row your Boat."

(Continued)

(Continued)

Spatial Intelligence

1. Visual aids such as manipulatives or representations of concepts (e.g., fractional parts) will assist spatial learners because they can often see the relationships.

2. As one variant, teachers may challenge groups of students in the class to write "a picture example of this problem."

Interpersonal Intelligence

1. Group work on math facts problems; have students debate mathematical intelligence points or concepts to each other; every 15 minutes during math class, the teacher could say, "Turn to your partner and explain that concept to each other. See if you both understand it the same way."

Bodily/Kinesthetic Intelligence

1. Movement along a number line on the floor during instruction on operations involving positive and negative integers is one example of a math movement activity.

2. Movement through an addition or subtraction math problem is another example. For the problem 6 + 8 = ? the teacher should have 6 students stand on one side of the room and 8 stand on the other side, then have the groups move together. This can be adapted to teach a "counting on" tactic. Begin with the group of 6 kids (because that number came first in the problem) and, one at a time, have the other students join the group while the teacher demonstrates "counting on" (e.g., begin with the number 6, and when the first student joins, say, "7," etc.—thus "counting on" from 6).

Clearly, this emphasis on varying strengths of students in these discrete intelligences will necessitate that teachers develop a larger variety of instructional activities in order to offer all students an opportunity to learn. This approach is particularly useful in the inclusive class (Katz et al., 2002). For students who do not have a strength in linguistic learning, or even logical/mathematical learning, various activities that involve other intelligences may result in the same level of mastery of the content. Thus, proponents of multiple intelligences instruction urge teachers to teach using a wide array of instructional tactics for mathematics.

SUMMARY OF BRAIN RESEARCH

With this emerging understanding of how brains function in learning math, some preliminary conclusions can be provided for teachers. The boxed text that follows provides a brief summary of the research on how the brain learns mathematics.

Summary of Brain Research on Mathematics Learning

1. *Basic counting is hardwired into the brain* and seems to be present at birth. This is a survival skill (e.g., how many animals are after me?), making this early math skill a high brain priority. Anything more complex is a much lower brain priority and requires formal or informal schooling.

2. *Mathematics involves a variety of brain areas* and thus is highly complex. The frontal lobe and parietal lobe—areas of the cerebrum—seem to be most heavily involved in math, but the visual cortex is involved also, suggesting that students may need to "visualize" math problems. Also, because mathematical skill is often dependent upon reading, the regions of the brain involved in the complex reading process are also often involved in mathematical tasks, including the angular gyrus, Wernicke's area, and Broca's area.

3. *Gender maturation within the brain may explain early achievement differences.* Brain research has documented that the brains of young boys mature faster in certain areas, including spatial and visual abilities, and this may explain why young boys seem to do better in math than young girls (Strauss, 2003).

4. *Motivation is critical to learning;* it provides an emotional rationale for learning new material. Errorless learning, scaffolded instruction, and charted progress reports motivate almost all students.

5. *Brains conceptualize mathematics in a variety of ways.* Because students may have varying strengths and weaknesses in several of the multiple intelligences (Gardner, 1993), teachers must develop an array of activities that address a variety of these intelligences. In short, teachers should be teaching the same content numerous times (Bender, 2002), in a variety of ways, using novel teaching approaches that capture students' attention, and offer a variety of learning opportunities tied to various intelligences.

6. *Brains seek patterns and "big ideas" in mathematics.* Because students learn best when presented with the same concept repeatedly in various contexts, the big ideas within the mathematics curriculum should be repeatedly stressed in different contexts.

Based on the research that has been undertaken, some preliminary guidelines for how teachers should conduct mathematical instruction may be provided. The following list of ten brain-compatible instructional guidelines should provide you with food for thought on how you teach math. Of course, these should be viewed merely as general guidelines; different students may require different approaches to instruction, based on their particular learning style.

TEACHING TACTICS

BRAIN-COMPATIBLE GUIDELINES FOR MATH INSTRUCTION

1. Less Is More. Students with math problems will master more if exposed to less. Teachers should adapt content in the math curriculum based on the needs and learning profiles of the students. Generally it is much more advisable to truly develop understanding of

(Continued)

(Continued)

a few problems rather than assign many problems. Also, some students may not be as successful as others in mastering problems in the same time frame. Fewer problems that are similar in structure and that allow students to develop deep understanding is preferable to many problems of varying types.

2. Present Information at Three Levels. New concepts in math should be presented at three levels: concrete (e.g., manipulatives), pictorial or representational, and abstract. Visualizing math problems through the use of concrete examples and/or representational examples assists many students in mastery at almost every grade level (Thompson, 1992). Manipulatives should be used across the grade levels for students with learning problems. Teachers should have students visualize problems using manipulatives and then explain the result to each other. Have other students develop a representation of the problem, while still others consider it abstractly. Have students consider the question, "How can we make math representational?" This will assist learners who have a strength in spatial intelligence.

3. Teach the "Big Ideas" in Mathematics. Teachers should assist students in searching for and emphasizing the big ideas in math that cut across problem types (Harniss et al., 2002; Wiggins & McThigh, 1998). We now know that brains seek patterns, or "shorthand ways of understanding," and our teaching should explicitly address these ideas.

4. Emphasize Mathematical Patterns. Using the patterns of counting by threes or fives can help with multiplication math facts. If possible, present patterns or steps in problem solution as an outline that remains posted on the wall for the entire unit. Use math patterns as classroom "games" with fluid, fun, "quick check" questions fired out to the class at various points in the day (Fuson & Wearne, 1997).

5. Teach Math Facts to a High Level of Automaticity. Students can proceed successfully in math only after the math facts are learned at a high level. The use of chants, music, and other novel teaching tactics will enhance memory for facts. These techniques are quite enjoyable, and will assist students who learn better via using their strengths in musical intelligence.

6. Use Novelty to Build on Students' Strengths. Novelty increases learning and allows you to present information in various ways. Make certain to identify three or more intelligences to address in the presentation of new information, and use novel teaching ideas to present that information. Use the learning styles/multiple intelligences concept to identify and teach to strengths. I suggest that on every day of instruction, teachers should develop some movement-based activity to represent concepts. For every graph or chart, teachers should find creative ways to represent the sections of the chart with bodily movements (touching the head, shaking the fingers, etc.). Alternatively, teachers may stand students in the positions of various math problems and then move them through the problem. Such novelty will enhance the learning and result in better retention.

7. Teach Algorithms Explicitly. Have students identify word problems that do and do not involve the same algorithms. Teachers should model both examples and nonexamples of the new concept. Further, teachers should emphasize concepts when correcting student work, and in this fashion assist students in developing a deep understanding of the concept. Research has clearly shown that merely informing students of their correctness or errors shows no positive effects on student learning (Gersten et al., 2002), so teachers should always strive to develop deep understandings, as encouraged by the NCTM standards.

8. Teach to Both Brain Hemispheres. While some math is hardwired into the frontal lobe and other left brain areas, other math requires spatial understanding and other right hemispheric functions. Teachers should build lesson plans to emphasize more right hemisphere involvement, since most classrooms are traditionally "left brain" oriented. Activities may include "visualization" activities, number chants, or rhythms (Sousa, 2001).

9. Scaffold the Student's Practice. Teachers should use real-world examples and provide scaffolded assistance to students throughout the learning process (various examples of scaffolding are presented later in this text). Applications of constructs should be emphasized in varying levels of complexity, using various authentic instructional and authentic assessment techniques. Teachers should make connections between student's prior knowledge and new concepts using real-world examples, as emphasized in the NCTM standards (Johnson, 2000). Also, use students to teach each other, to summarize main points, and to tutor each other in new concepts in short (e.g., five-minute) tutoring lessons. These types of activities will enhance student motivation to learn math as well as stress interpersonal learning activities.

10. Understand the Fear and Explore the Beauty. Many students fear mathematics (Montague, 1997) because they may remember early failures, and this negative "affective response" to mathematics can be quite debilitating. Teachers should intentionally plan activities that assist students in developing a more positive response to mathematics (Montague, 1997). For example, teachers may offer error-free learning practices or buddy-learning activities that may remove some embarrassment from periodic failures. Also, many students study math for years without having a Gestalt or excitement-in-learning experience. Showing the beauty of math patterns can be quite satisfying for a naturalistic-oriented person. It is the patterns, the constructs, the logical progression of algorithms that make math like music—a symphony to share with students.

SOURCES: Geller & Smith, 2002; Gersten et al., 2002; Harniss et al., 2002; Johnson, 2000; Montague, 1997; Thompson, 1992; Sousa, 2001.

Web Site Review: Brain-Compatible Instruction and Multiple Intelligences

There are literally hundreds of Web sites that address brain-compatible instruction and/or multiple intelligences, and only a few can be presented here. You could easily do a Google search on "brain-compatible instruction/math" or on "multiple intelligences" and find numerous Web sites.

Still, this list and the links on these pages will get you started.

http://school.discovery.com/brainboosters

This Web site ties brain-compatible instruction and math together and presents a large number of mathematical brainteasers. Each presents a problem as number play. In using this site, some math teachers have presented a brainteaser at the begining of each period, as students are coming into the classroom, and have had students share their answers as they finish the period.

www.brainconnection.com

This site presents periodic articles by some of the leaders in the brain-compatible research field, such as Robert Sylwester, PhD. While the site is related to a marketing site for a brain-compatible reading program, useful information is often presented in these monthly articles, and many additional links may be found here.

www.ldrc.ca/projects/miinventory

This location is the site for the learning disabilities resource community, and provides some good information on multiple intelligences (MI). I like this site because it provides a printable, informal inventory that teachers can use with their students to roughly determine the various multiple intelligence strengths of each student. That is a great activity to introduce the concept of MI to your students.

www.Campbell.k12.ky.us

This is the Web site for the Campbell County School District in Kentucky. That district has begun a districtwide initiative on "Building Better Brains." Professional development activities are tied to that effort, as are the district's efforts to improve test scores in a variety of areas. This site shows that a well led, determined school district can create a very positive environment for exciting learning based on the very latest information on how brains learn.

INSTRUCTIONAL PHASES FOR DEVELOPING MATH SKILLS

Stepping Stones to Number Sense

Because the early development of number sense is so critical to success in math, several researchers have investigated number sense, and some teaching guidelines for development number sense are available today. For example, Gersten and Chard (1999) identified several levels of number sense among children with difficulty in math. These researchers likened the construct of "number sense" in mathematics to the concept of "phoneme instruction" in reading. Within the past decade, research has demonstrated conclusively that "phoneme manipulation" skills—that is, the ability to recognize and intentionally manipulate different speech sounds—represent a more fundamental and earlier prerequisite skill for reading than "phonics" (i.e., letter shapes/sound skills). Of course, phonics had, for the past four decades, been the first step in reading instruction; only now have teachers realized that phoneme manipulation skills are a prerequisite to phonics. In short, if students cannot detect and manipulate sounds independent of letter recognition, they cannot succeed in phonics, which associates different sounds with specific letters. To pursue this comparison a bit farther, the concept of number sense may be as fundamental in learning mathematics as phoneme instruction has become in learning to read (Gersten & Chard, 1999).

> In short, without number sense, the child may never succeed in math at even the lowest levels, since concepts such as numeration, addition, or subtraction would have no substantive meaning. Clearly, development of number sense is a critically important first step in math instruction.

Gersten and Chard (1999) identified several stepping-stones that allow teachers to evaluate a child's understanding of number sense. These stepping-stones represent increasingly complex levels of a child's understanding of number sense.

Stepping-Stones for Number Sense Development

Level 1

Children at this level have not yet developed number sense or show any knowledge of relative quantity. A child at this level will not be able to answer questions involving "more than" or "less than." Further, children at this level would not have the basic concepts of fewer or greater.

Level 2

Children at this level are beginning to acquire number sense. A child here would be able to state and understand terms like "lots," "five," and "ten." These children also are beginning to understand the concepts of "more than" and "less than." These children do not understand basic computation skills, but they do understand greater/lesser amounts.

Level 3

Children at this level fully understand "more than" and "less than." They also have a general understanding of computation and may use a "count up from one" strategy to solve problems. These children may use their fingers or manipulate objects to solve a problem. While these children are beginning to understand computation, there will still be many errors in counting. For children at this level, adding four and three may involve holding up four fingers on one hand and three on the other. They will start at one and count to four, and then look at the other hand, and count from one to three. Finally they will count all of the fingers together to get an answer. Errors are seen more often when the child is calculating numbers higher than five, because these computations involve using fingers on both hands.

(Continued)

(Continued)

Level 4

Children at this level use a more sophisticated "count up" or "counting on" process, rather than the "counting all" process just described. For example, these children may hold up fingers to represent each addend, begin with the number of the first addend, and then "count on" to the second. For adding four and three, the student starts at four and adds the three, using fingers and counting out loud: "Four, five, six, seven." At this level the child can keep track of the first addend while counting to the second. Thus, these children understand the conceptual reality of numbers (i.e., they do not have to count to four to know that four exists). Children at this level may not even need to use their fingers or manipulatives to count to find a solution. Children at this level can solve any digit problem presented to them, provided they can count accurately.

Level 5

Children at this level are at the highest level of number sense. They can use a retrieval strategy. They can respond quickly and correctly, pulling from memory the answer to a problem. They have learned addition math facts to a highly automatic level and have memorized some basic subtraction facts. These children can recall that $4 + 3 = 7$. They can also turn the fact around to state that $7 - 3 = 4$.

With these stepping-stones in mind, teachers need strategies for developing number sense in children, including older children, perhaps throughout the elementary school years. The section below describes several activities that early education teachers can use for teaching number sense. These activities will improve the number sense of students who already have the basics. Further, these tactics will help students with deficits in number sense to catch up with other students.

Mathematical Play to Develop Number Sense

A number of strategies have been suggested for developing number sense, and many of these are based on informal games and mathematical play for students (Checkley, 1999; Griffin et al., 2003; Gurganus, 2004; Whitenack et al., 2002). Initially, teachers should emphasize mathematical terms as "play" in the typical routines of the classroom; a number of ideas for this informal instruction in the early grades are presented below.

TEACHING TACTICS

TEN INFORMAL TACTICS TO DEVELOP NUMBER SENSE

1. Pair Numbers With Objects. In the class routine, when discussing objects in the class or pictures in a storybook, pair numbers and objects. For example, there are two wheels on a bicycle, three wheels on a tricycle, and four wheels on a car. Students will thus begin to associate numbers with different values rather than merely as labels (Gurganus, 2004).

2. Begin Class With Counting. Even young children can typically count to ten, and choral counting out loud emphasizes counting without the embarrassment of being wrong (e.g., "Let's count together how many objects are on this shelf in the front of the class"). After a few days of counting, pair the counting with written numbers on the dry erase board.

3. Extend Counting to Other Number Patterns. In some of the early counting activities, students should extend their counting to other, larger numbers. Rather than counting from one to ten, teachers could have students count from 101 to 110 (Gurganus, 2004).

4. Use Finger Patterns. Finger patterns are a way children use their fingers to represent the numbers one through ten (Whitenack et al., 2002). Provide students varied exercises that allow them to represent the numbers with their fingers. Students at first only use their fingers the same way they have learned how to count. Part of number sense is recognizing that there are several different ways to represent numbers, and playing games with finger patterns allows children to think unconventionally. Students need the exercises to see that three fingers on one hand and two fingers on the other hand represent the same number as five fingers on one hand. Class discussion during the finger pattern game allows students to see the differences and the similarities between the different ways of representing numbers. Having students explain why they picked three fingers on one hand and two fingers on the other lets the students that held up five fingers on one hand see a new pattern and visa versa. This is a good type of instruction to use in a "buddy" game, where kids are paired together to generate an alternative solution.

5. Plan Estimation Experiences. Discuss "less than" and "more than" with students and encourage estimation. Some students are uncomfortable with estimation since students typically strive for the "right" answer. Encourage students to provide an estimation within a certain range (e.g., "How many shoes are in class today? Give me a number between forty and seventy," or "How many students are sitting in a single group in the media center?").

6. Counting-Off in Line. Students in lower grades frequently line up to go to the lunchroom or elsewhere. Every time students line up, teachers could encourage them to count off, and thus stress number sense (Griffin et al., 2003). As an interesting variation in the upper grades, have students count off when in line using a "quiet voice" but have each person who is a multiple of a certain number (say a multiple of five) say his or her number louder. This makes learning multiplication more interesting since multiples will be frequently used in the classroom.

7. Stress Numbers in Other Subjects. When encountering a number in a reading story, take a few moments to explore the number. When a group of characters in a story does something together, stop for a moment and say, "I want to get a sense of how many are doing that in this story. Let's have students in the first row stand up to represent that number."

8. Emphasize Measurement. From the early days of kindergarten, teachers should take measurements of objects and discuss them with the class. Teachers may use a short tape measure to measure the length of the teacher's desk or a student's desktop. When measuring distances on the floor, teachers may add the element of counting steps (e.g., "How many steps are there in the ten feet between the front row of student desks and the

(Continued)

(Continued)

teacher's desk?" Have a student walk that distance and count his or her steps. Next, the teacher would measure another floor space of ten feet in a different area of the classroom, and ask the class how many steps the same student would use to cover that distance).

9. Chart Making Money. Using charted data in higher grades (which takes only one or two minutes at the beginning of the class period) can encourage students to use numbers in a real-world environment. A teacher might start each student with $1,000 in make-believe money in the stock market, and have each student pick stocks to buy and to chart stock price changes for. This can be a fun learning activity with real-world significance.

10. Model Enjoyment of Numbers. Perhaps the most important legacy a teacher can leave with a student is enjoyment of number play. Gurganus (2004) emphasizes the importance of the teacher modeling the enjoyment of numbers and establishing a climate for curiosity in mathematics.

TEACHING STRATEGY: MATHEMATICAL GAMES TO DEVELOP NUMBER SENSE

In addition to the informal tactics noted above, other more structured mathematical games and activities can also assist in developing number sense. Generally, these will be more effective if this instruction is managed as mathematical play, rather than instruction. Teachers should be creative with these general ideas. In using these mathematical play activities, it is critical that teachers develop the theme or "big idea" that they wish to teach, and emphasize that theme repeatedly. Teachers should summarize each problem by talking with the students about the problems. Teachers may make summary statements about work completed by the students. Statements such as, "If you add, then the amount you finish with is larger than what you started with" will assist students in developing number sense (Griffin et al., 2003).

TEACHING TACTICS

GAMES AND ACTIVITIES TO DEVELOP NUMBER SENSE

1. "Catch the Teacher" Games. Teachers may occasionally wish to make mistakes and have students point out these counting mistakes. This is a tactic that can work for students in a variety of grade levels. For example, teachers may skip numbers or repeat numbers while counting and instruct the students to quietly raise their hands if they hear a mistake. Students must then describe the mistake that the teacher made (Griffin et al., 2003).

2. Greater/Fewer Games. Students who need to learn the concepts of greater or fewer can generally be taught using manipulatives such as the same-size blocks, papers with dots, and the like. Having the students line up and each take a different number of steps may assist students to see relationships between numbers (e.g., that a student who took four steps went farther than a student who took two steps). Teachers should use several different methods that students will be able to understand to concretely illustrate various number facts, such as the fact that seven is always greater than four. For example, teachers should use different-size blocks to illustrate the same number concept (e.g., seven is greater than four regardless of the size of block).

As an example of a number sense activity for older children, teachers may challenge the students with questions such as the following:

> I have ten candy bars. We'll just pretend my fingers are candy bars. Here are some candy bars in this hand. (The teacher should hold up four fingers, while hiding the other hand behind his or her back.) How many am I hiding from you?

3. Moving on Down the Road. Using a number line on the floor, have students move "down the road" by noting the numbers as they pass. Emphasize that six steps are more than five steps, and so on. For older students, this number line activity can be done with both positive and negative integers.

4. Teaching Puppets. Teachers can teach beginning addition and help increase number sense at the same time. Using a puppet, the teacher would place a specific number of cookies in a bag (e.g., three cookies). Next the teacher would have a student draw a card from a pile that has "+ 2," "– 3," or "+ 4," or other such number facts on it. The teacher should ask groups of students to think through the problem and then do the problem using the puppet by calculating how many cookies are left. This can assist spatial learners as well as students with a strength in interpersonal intelligence.

5. Pocket Games for One-to-One Correspondence. Use a hanging shoe bag with at least ten pockets (Checkley, 1999) and put a different number on each pocket. Give students cards that have varying numbers of objects on them. Have the students match the number and the card by placing the card in the appropriately labeled pocket. Students may even make their own cards.

6. Snap-Together Objects. Kindergarten and first graders need to practice addition and subtraction repeatedly in various game formats. Teachers may use a group of cubes or objects that snap together to assist in this practice. First, divide the students into groups of two. Next, give each group a chain of ten snap-together objects. Then, one student should break the chain and give the other student the portion of the chain that is left. The second student would then be required to tell how many objects are missing (Checkley, 1999). This will assist bodily/kinesthetic learners.

7. Using Mathematical Models. Allow students to make mathematical models for the problems they are asked to solve. For example, consider the following problem: "There are seven children; how many eyes are there?" Teachers may wish to allow the students to create their own drawing for this problem in order to help them find a solution—a technique that will be of great benefit to visual/spatial learners. Some students may just draw a circle with two dots. Other students will draw more elaborate drawings that have noses and mouths. In this approach, the students are allowed to use their creativity to solve math problems (Checkley, 1999).

(Continued)

(Continued)

8. Use Manipulatives. Many students unfortunately feel that blocks or other manipulatives are "baby toys," and some students even put them away by first or second grade. For other students, however, manipulatives need to be used for as long as possible in the early grades. When students ask about manipulatives, point out that almost all teachers are using sections of a round pie for fractions in Grades 3 and 4, and even Grade 5. Also, teachers should not insist on students' using pictures or "representations of manipulatives" before they are ready. Rather, use of manipulatives should be allowed for as long as students wish in the early grades (Checkley, 1999).

9. Make a Class Quilt. This is a creative activity that is great for spatial learners. First, each student designs his or her own "square" for the quilt. Teachers may wish to use crayons or tempera paint to color the squares of cloth. The squares are then combined and sewn together to make a quilt. This allows students an early introduction to geometry, fractions, visual-spatial reasoning, and addition, since the quilt components represent various shapes and various portions of the whole. Teachers should display or use the quilt so the students will be reminded of the concepts as well as have pride in their work (Checkley, 1999).

10. Musical Fraction Squares. In this "musical squares" game, the parts of a fraction can be demonstrated. Begin with four students and four chairs and write "4/4" on the dry erase board. Discuss the fact that the chairs represent the numerator and the students represent the denominator. Thus, if the teacher removes one chair while the music plays, there will be 3/4 or three chairs and four students. The teacher can then discuss various fractions with the students and talk about, "What is left when the music ends?" or "What has been taken away?"

TEACHING STRATEGY: PLANNING FOR MULTIPLE INTELLIGENCES

Putting the Ideas Together

In addition to understanding the brain bases for mastery in mathematics, teachers need to develop a repertoire of instructional skills to make number sense and mathematical play a characteristic of the classroom. A variety of additional ideas for this are presented below.

TEACHING TACTICS

TEN TACTICS FOR PROVIDING INITIAL INSTRUCTION IN MATH

1. Movement as a Learning Tool. For any math problems that can be represented by specific locations (e.g., components of a frequency chart, comparisons of geometric shapes, various distributions, etc.), teachers should develop an activity that involves movement around the classroom. Brain research has shown that movement will enhance memory for almost every child, and it provides a novel teaching technique. Many teachers of young children frequently use movement, but the use of movement is highly recommended for learners at all ages. The musical fraction squares game described earlier presents one idea for movement. As another example, when teaching various bar graphs, stand the students in the shape of each bar (e.g., three students make a shorter line than five students, etc.).

Remember that any concept that can be graphically represented on an overhead or on the dry erase board can be a model for students. Merely have students stand in that same configuration and then discuss why it is important that they be so placed in the overall chart of the concept.

2. Cross Out Problems. This approach to practice work can assist children who have attention problems. On a page of math problems, the teacher may instruct the student to cross out every other problem to adjust the assignment for these kids. This adaptation emphasizes the less-is-more aspect of teaching kids with learning problems, since some students find looking at an entire page of math problems quite daunting. Crossing out some of the problems may make the work seem possible.

3. Peer Buddies. After the teaching phase of the math lesson, when some students are doing reteaching work, the teacher may wish to have students do math problems together as peer buddies. This involves having two students work together on the same set of problems. This can alleviate some embarrassment, since it is more fun to work together and each student can "assist" the other. This will be a great teaching strategy for students with a strength in interpersonal intelligence.

4. Color Coding Cue Words. Color highlights novelty in learning and results in increased attention from the learning brains within the classroom. Teachers should use colored markers frequently. For example, in subtraction problems the teacher may wish to color subtrahends a specific color. Further, in word problems, teachers may color the "cue words" that usually specify one operation or another. On math worksheets that involve several types of problems (e.g., adding fractions with like or unlike denominators), teachers may color code the problems of one type or another (e.g., like-denominator problems all in red, and unlike-denominator problems all in black). This will assist students in recognizing the types of problems.

5. Teach With Edibles. For younger kids, using an individual supply of edibles (fruits such as raisins work well here) can make using manipulative counters more fun! Use edibles as the counters, and after each correct problem, the student can eat one of the counters. The child's lesson is finished when the edibles in his or her pile are gone!

6. A Chart/Teaming Activity. The teacher begins by dividing the class into teams. At a signal from the teacher, one member of each team runs to the team's chart to write a relevant fact on the chart about that topic. The other team members should make certain the fact is correct. At the next signal, the next team member writes down another fact. This activity involves movement and cooperation among team members as well as competition between the teams.

7. Personal Learning Timelines. Each student should keep a timeline, illustrated with pictures of the types of problems he or she was working on at various dates during the year. This can be quite motivating for students, who see their progress in mathematics. These timelines should also be shared with parents at various points in the school year.

(Continued)

(Continued)

8. Math Facts Call-Outs. Teachers begin this activity by dividing the class into four teams and having the teams line up in rows. Then the teacher calls out math facts problems for one member of the first team. If that member calls out the math fact correctly, the team gets two points. If he or she needs help from a team member to get the math fact right, the team gets one point. If that person gets a math fact wrong, the team gets no points. This will assist in learning math facts at a high level of automaticity.

9. Use a Math Portfolio. Teachers may wish to save a series of worksheets, activities, and group projects in which a child has participated. As a guideline, teachers should save one assignment each week throughout the year. This portfolio can provide a critically important indicator of how a child is doing in math and, like the timelines above, can be shared with the child's parents or even with the child's teacher for the next year.

10. Use Multiplication Charts. Beginning at the top left of a sheet of paper, form a multiplication chart by writing the numbers 1–12 on both the horizontal and vertical axis. Then write the products at each intersection. Note for the students how they may find products (e.g., lay two sheets of paper across the lines, and the intersection of the papers shows the product of any two numbers). Also note that the rows represent the same as "count by . . ." for each number in the chart.

SOURCES: Bender, 2002; Forsten, Grant, & Hollas, 2002.

Further, in addition to understanding these basics of instruction in math, teachers need a clear concept of what differentiated instruction in math is. While volumes of texts can be (and have been) written that detail a wide variety of specific mathematical instructional strategies, teachers need to develop a deeper understanding than most of the "lists of good teaching ideas" that books present. Rather, teachers need to understand how the various instructional ideas and tactics fit together to form a coherent instructional approach for differentiation in the math curriculum.

This chapter has provided a basis in both multiple intelligences and brain-compatible instruction in order for teachers to have a better understanding of the differentiated instructional strategies that may be used for all students in the elementary classroom. Further, in order to get a clear understanding of differentiation, teachers may wish to use a self-evaluation tool that involves many of the basics of brain-compatible instruction in the act of lesson planning. One option for teachers is a lesson planning grid that cross-references multiple intelligences and the levels of instruction, as presented in Figure 1.2.

Teachers should copy this figure and use it in their lesson planning for mathematics. In fact, this tool can be of assistance when planning an instructional unit at any level. Imagine the following example for teaching students in the early grades how to tell time. In this unit of instruction teachers should strive to design activities that address each of the areas of the self-evaluation grid. For example, consider the mix of activities for instruction in telling time found on p. 24.

REPRESENTATIONAL LEVELS		
	Concrete	Pictorial	Abstract
Bodily/Kinesthetic			
Musical			
Spatial			
Inter/Intrapersonal			
Naturalistic			
Linguistic			
Logical/Mathematical			

Figure 1.2   A Self-Evaluation Grid for Lesson Planning

IDEAS FROM TEACHERS

Ideas to Teach Telling Time

Clock Face Movement Activities

Teachers should prepare a large clock face (perhaps six feet in diameter) on the floor, using masking tape to make the circle, and placing digits 1 through 12 in the appropriate spots. A meter stick may be used as the minute hand and a ruler as the hour hand. Students, working in teams of two or three, should be required to display various times on the large clock by moving the hands as necessary; they may be told, "Make the clock say 1:20." In order to assure involvement of all students, each student should hold a small clock face and individually complete the same task when a team of students is working on the large clock face.

Musical Intelligence/Repetition

Couple the activity above with the use of the song below, to the tune of "The Wheels on the Bus Go Round and Round."

The short hand says its number first,

Number first, number first.

The short hand says its number first,

When we're telling time.

The long hand is tall and counts by five,

Counts by five, counts by five.

The long hand is tall and counts by five,

When we're telling time.

A Number Line of Fives

Much of telling time involves increments of five minutes, so students need to be able to count by fives. To facilitate that, teachers can create a large number line across the top of the dry erase board, with every multiple of five printed in red and other numbers printed in black or blue. Student who cannot yet count by fives can merely read the numbers printed in red.

Web Site Review: Telling Time Instruction

The Web site below has a wide variety of math activities, and it particularly includes the option to print out worksheets that present a clock face and require the students to draw hands on the picture. While there, investigate the many other options for instruction mathematics in a wide variety of areas.

http://math.about.com

In the set of simple activities earlier, a series of differentiated teaching tactics have been used that are novel and address a variety of multiple intelligences. Specifically, the activities address bodily/kinesthetic learning in a concrete fashion, through movement across the floor, as well as the students' manipulating their own clock faces. Spatial intelligence is addressed concretely in the spatial aspect of clock face manipulation. Linguistic skill is emphasized in the use of the song, as is musical intelligence. Interpersonal intelligence is involved in the teamwork aspect of the clock face activity. Also, a variety of big ideas are addressed, including aggregation of data and numeration.

Further, when an activity includes a concrete example, as have these tactics, and teachers have thoroughly discussed the example, then both representational and abstract learning have also taken place. Thus, after such instruction, teachers can draw an arrow across the grid from left to right for each of these intelligences, since instruction has been offered at each level. Finally, many of these activities (e.g., the song and the large clock face activity) could be repeated several times in this instructional unit of telling time.

Note that while concrete examples will, of necessity, include both a representational and an abstract component, the inverse is not true. That is, abstract examples do not necessarily include concrete and/or representational components. Rather, teachers offering abstract instruction should devise and employ a variety of additional techniques that will offer concrete or representational levels of instruction on the same "big idea."

WHAT'S NEXT?

In the next chapter we will cover some of the basics of differentiation in mathematics lessons and explore how teachers can plan effective mathematics instructional lessons based on these differentiated instructional concepts.

Planning for Differentiated Math Instruction

2

Strategies in this chapter include the following:

- Direct Instruction Lesson Planning
- Guess, Assess, and Tear Out
- Results of Guess, Assess, and Tear Out

FROM DIRECT INSTRUCTION TO DIFFERENTIATED INSTRUCTION

As discussed in Chapter 1, differentiated instruction involves more than mere application of effective teaching ideas that address a wider variety of multiple intelligences. In fact, differentiated instruction represents a drastic paradigm shift that fundamentally changes the way teachers teach mathematics (as well as other subjects) across the elementary school curriculum.

Teachers who wish to develop a differentiated classroom for math instruction must begin in the lesson-planning phase. For the past 30 years, lesson planning has been based on a body of research that was known as the "effective schools" research of the 1970s (Bender, 1996). Other names for this research movement include "direct instruction," "mastery learning," and "effective teacher behaviors." All of these involve highly developed lesson plans designed to maximize instruction time or "engaged" time in which the student was cognitively engaged with the content (see Bender, 1996, for a discussion of effective teaching behaviors and direct instruction). In some examples of direct instruction, scripted lessons were used in which teachers literally read a prepared script while teaching (Bender, 1996).

> Such highly structured direct instruction lessons were possible in classes that involved only a small number of children and a small range of academic diversity.

For our purposes, we'll use the term *direct instruction* to represent this type of instructional approach. Today, our lesson planning and even our way of thinking about math instruction stems from this body of research, and most teacher's manuals in most math curricula are written in terms of this direct instructional approach.

Of course, to understand direct instruction we must consider the setting of the research on direct instruction. Specifically, researchers of the 1960s and 1970s based their work on the types of classrooms and the types of students who were then prevalent in the public schools. For example, if a teacher taught in Grade 5 in the early 1970s, he or she could realistically assume that most of the students in that class were working on reading and math somewhere between grade level 3 and grade level 7. In other words, while there were some differences in the children's math or reading skills, there was a fairly narrow level of academic diversity within the class. Much of the effective schools research took place in classrooms prior to the full implementation of Public Law 94-142; thus many students with special needs were excluded from much of this research.

In contrast, in today's fifth-grade class it is quite likely that students' achievement levels in reading and math range from grade level 1 up through grade level 10 or 11. Our nation has made a commitment to educate all students, and today's teachers face that fact daily. Thus, while there was limited academic diversity in the classes of the 1970s, the levels of academic diversity noted in the typical classroom today in the 21st century were unheard of in the 1970s. In spite of this increase in the range of academic skills present in the typical classroom, educators have not effectively reconceptualized how teachers should conduct math lessons to meet the demands of this level of diversity.

Today, modern mathematics curricula have highly developed lesson plans that employ the direct instruction teaching phases. These are almost always presented in the teacher's manual in some form. Yet, if the range of the students' mathematics skills in today's classrooms has changed, it may be time to adjust our thinking about how to structure our lessons and lesson-planning activities. Again, Tomlinson's (1999) work on the differentiated classroom represents a fairly drastic paradigm change in how teachers should lead their mathematics instruction. This chapter will explore this paradigm change in order to assist teachers in formulating a truly differentiated lesson plan.

> Because math curricula today present lesson plans in the direct instruction format, our task here will be to modify that lesson format into a set of differentiated instructional activities.

Thus, the lesson-planning job in mathematics becomes an exercise in planning the activities for various groups of students in the class who do not need to follow the traditional direct instruction lesson or who need an alternative lesson format.

TEACHING PHASES IN THE DIRECT INSTRUCTION LESSON

The traditional direct instruction lesson plan would typically present a series of instructional phases that were originally referred to as the "direct instruction" steps. These phases of learning, as enumerated in the effective schools research of the 1970s, have become the steps in the typical lesson plan in schools today (Bender, 1996). Presented below are the usual steps in direct instruction, and the types of instructional activities involved in each phase of instruction. While the terms may change from one math curriculum to another (some math curricula use "activate their understanding" rather than "orientation to the lesson," for example), teachers have planned their instruction for the past 30 years around these phases of the instructional lesson.

Steps in a Direct Instruction Lesson

Orientation to the Lesson

- Gain students' attention
- Relate today's lesson to a previously related lesson
- Use essential questions to activate students' thinking

Initial Instruction

- Teacher leads completion of several sample problems
- Teacher models and has students' model problem completion
- Teacher points out difficult aspects of problem

Teacher-Guided Practice

- Students complete problems under teacher supervision
- Teacher monitors each student's success in problem completion
- Teacher assists students independently
- Students may discuss problems with each other

Independent Practice

- Students complete sample problems independently
- Students may complete homework as independent practice

Check

- Teacher checks student performance on independent work

Reteach

- Teacher identifies students with continuing difficulty and reteaches the skills

The initial and fundamental assumptions behind the direct instruction lesson format were that all students would follow this main line of instructional activities and that this sequence would facilitate learning for all students. Of course, this assumed a relatively small level of academic diversity; for example, in order for this type of group instruction to work, one had to assume that students in Grade 5 were functioning somewhere around the Grade 5 level in mathematics—say between grade levels 3 and 6. It also assumed that all students could and would learn in the same fashion if the teacher presented an appropriate lesson based on high levels of engagement on the part of every student.

PROBLEMS WITH DIRECT INSTRUCTION IN A LARGE CLASS

As Tomlinson (1999) stated so succinctly, the increasing diversity of students, of learning styles, and of learning needs in the general education classroom has effectively outdated the set of assumptions on which direct instruction is based. In today's typical fifth-grade classroom, the high range of academic diversity makes it impossible for a teacher to teach effectively using only one instructional format.

In fact, the direct instructional format has never truly worked for many students within the class (i.e., typical classes including perhaps 25 or 30 students). For advanced students in those mathematics classes, this instructional sequence often leads to boredom in the early steps on any particular type of problem, since many advanced or gifted students may already have mastered the lesson prior to the teacher's initial instruction. Thus, those students would tend to be off-task by the time the teacher begins the later phases of the instructional lesson, and they might even begin to disrupt others in the class.

For students with less ability in the typical inclusive classroom, this model of instruction often failed to engage them because they may not have had the prerequisite skills necessary for the lesson. Consequently, many of those students demonstrate both off-task and disruptive behaviors, since they are bored with material that they cannot learn and are not engaged with the lesson activities. Therefore, as a result of teachers' attempting to follow this series of direct instructional steps, many students in the typical class were bored and often misbehaved, and of course managing those problems takes the teacher's time away from delivery of the lesson activity to the other students in the class.

Clearly, for today's diverse group of students, we will need to modify this direct instructional model considerably in order to differentiate the lesson and to increase the variety of activities in this class, if we wish to engage all learners in the mathematics content. While various theorists have provided such models of curriculum and lesson reorganization (e.g., Wiggins & McTighe, 1998), Tomlinson's (1999) differentiated instructional model seems to offer the most effective option.

TEACHING STRATEGY: THE GUESS, ASSESS, AND TEAR OUT TACTIC

The Guess, Assess, and Tear Out Tactic provides one way to modify the direct instructional lesson phases for increased differentiation in the class.

In using the Guess, Assess, and Tear Out idea, the teacher would begin the lesson-planning process with the first step as suggested by the direct instruction model described above—orientation to the lesson. After each instructional step in the traditional lesson, however, the teacher would do three things:

1. *Guess* which students have the concept,

2. *Assess* those several students with one or two quick questions, and

3. *Tear Out* of the class a small instructional group of those students who will perform an alternative instructional activity.

The Guess, Assess, and Tear Out Tactic is a lesson-planning approach that allows teachers to use the traditional direct instructional steps delineated above as the basis for instructional planning, while increasing the variety of activities offered for students who need alternative instructional approaches because of their diverse learning needs.

In this model of instruction, the terms *guess* and *assess* are self-explanatory. The teacher is (based on his or her judgment and previous experience with the students) guessing which students may have grasped the concept. Next, the teacher will quickly "assess" them informally, perhaps with a question such as, "Do you understand this idea?"

The final term above requires a bit more explanation. I've used the term *tear out* deliberately, since forming more than one or two instructional groups in a classroom early in the lesson is quite difficult for many teachers. While teachers have been using instructional groups for many years during the independent practice phase of the lesson, in a differentiated class these instructional groups will be formed much sooner in the lesson and much more frequently. In a differentiated class, teachers will form instructional groups even before they have presented the initial instruction in the topic to the class, and will form many more instructional groups than in traditional direct instructional teaching.

Because most of today's teachers were trained in the direct instructional teaching model, the modification of this standard lesson plan in order to differentiate the math activities in the classroom may be one of the most challenging aspects of the model. In short, one of the most difficult things to encourage teachers to do is to form multiple instructional groups that will be less supervised by the teacher, since using three or four groups of students in the classroom means that teachers must assume that students can learn from each other without such instructional supervision. This idea requires some degree of faith on the part of teachers who have not been prepared for this type of teaching.

Also, students as well as teachers are generally not well prepared for this type of instruction. While learning collaboratively from one's peers during the performance of an assigned task is certainly one requirement in the modern workplace, the direct instructional teaching model is rather authoritarian and doesn't provide ample opportunity for such peer mediated learning. Thus, providing students with increased opportunities to learn content from each other in settings that are somewhat less supervised by the teacher can result in enhanced instruction for a modern world. However, both teachers and students will need some experimental learning in order to function well within this model. Perhaps a concrete example will demonstrate this concept.

A DIFFERENTIATED INSTRUCTION LESSON EXAMPLE

In order to demonstrate the Guess, Assess, and Tear Out approach, imagine the following instructional lesson in Ms. Adrian's third-grade math class. The class includes 22 students, five of whom are special education students, and two of those students have attention deficit disorders coupled with high levels of hyperactivity. In schools today, this would seem to be a typical class. In this scenario, Ms. Adrian is teaching a math lesson concerning the aggregation of data, the creation of a tally table, and the eventual formulation of a frequency table summarizing those data.

As an advance organizer of the Guess, Assess, and Tear Out technique, the chart below shows a comparison of the direct instruction phases of this lesson and a differentiated lesson plan for the same lesson. Note the direct instruction activities appear on the left of the chart, and the types of "tear out" activities suggested by the Guess, Assess, and Tear Out Tactic are noted on the right-hand side of the chart.

TEACHING STRATEGY: USING GUESS, ASSESS, AND TEAR OUT! MOVING FROM DIRECT INSTRUCTION TO DIFFERENTIATED INSTRUCTION IN MATH

Direct Instruction Phases of Learning	Differentiated Instruction Guess, Assess, and Tear-Out Activities
I. Orientation • Cover tally tables and frequency tables	• After the intro, break out one group (Omega group) to create a tally table on the floor, then rejoin main group
II. Initial Instruction • Teach tally tables and frequency tables	• Tear out a second group (the Beta group, using examples from the text) • Beta group to use the tally table on the floor for some sample problems
III. Teacher Guided Practice • Have mainline group complete practice worksheet	• Have Omega and Beta groups evaluate each other's work • Tear out another group if necessary
IV. Independent Practice • Have students complete the independent practice	• Omega and Beta groups move into other enrichment activities

V. Check

- Have Omega and Beta groups describe their activities to the entire class; continue to check comprehension

VI. Reteach

- Reteach the concepts to a smaller group of kids who haven't mastered it

- Use members of Omega and Beta groups to "buddy up" with students who need help

To begin this lesson with an attention-grabbing orientation activity, Ms. Adrian might ask students to identify their favorite dinosaur, since dinosaurs have become big Hollywood stars recently. She would hold up a picture of one of the five most recognizable dinosaurs and have a student at the dry erase board begin to tally how many students like the T-Rex, the allosaurus, the raptor, or the stegosaurus. Once she has several sets of tally marks on the dry erase board, she may then say something like, "How can we summarize these data so they make sense?" Ms. Adrian may ask for suggestions from the class, but she will eventually show a frequency table that looks something like the following.

Tally Table and Frequency Table for Dinosaur Preferences

Dinosaurs	Tally Count	Frequency

After this brief orientation activity, the traditional direct instruction lesson would suggest that Ms. Adrian begin to teach about tally tables, and ultimately frequency tables, using several similar examples. The differentiated lesson plan, however, offers another approach. For example, it is possible that, after the orientation to the lesson, and prior to initial instruction, some of the students have already mastered the concept. During the orientation phase of the lesson, several students may have looked ahead in the text and seen several examples of how to tally data in table form, and then generated a frequency table from the tally marks. In short, even before the lesson is taught some students may already have grasped the idea and may need a more challenging lesson.

At this point, the Guess, Assess, and Tear Out technique offers an alternative. After the orientation to the lesson, rather than beginning the initial instruction for everyone in the class, Ms. Adrian should use the Guess, Assess, and Tear Out Tactic. Prior to any actual teacher led instruction, it is possible—in fact it is likely in most heterogeneous classes in today's schools—that Ms. Adrian could identify some students who have already mastered the concept. In other words, some of the more advanced students do not even need to be taught the lesson. Ms. Adrian would identify three to five students by educated guess and a quick assessment question or two directed to the group. Questions such as, "Do you think you could structure a tally table to collect data, and then transfer those data to a frequency table?" For the students who indicate they could, she should tear out these students and provide some group work as an alternative instructional activity.

> The Guess, Assess, and Tear Out Tactic offers the opportunity to provide "tiered instruction" or instruction on the same content but at slightly different cognitive levels for different groups of students. The provision of tiered lessons is one fundamental element of a differentiated instructional lesson.

Let's follow the next part of the lesson for a moment from the perspective of that tear-out group, by exploring the group's tiered activity assignment.

THE OMEGA GROUP

We'll call these students the Omega Group—the first group of students torn out of the mainline instruction. Of course, you may use any terms you like to name these groups, as long as the names for the groups are nonsequential and thus do not indicate a qualitative judgment on the skills or the intellect of the group. For the first activity of the Omega Group, Ms. Adrian may hand them a preselected assignment sheet for a group work activity involving structuring such a frequency table. These five students would then be instructed to move to a separate section of the room to begin their group project.

In a differentiated lesson, the good news is that teachers usually don't have to create these alternative activities; these group project alternatives are usually described in the teacher's manual as "enrichment" activities or "reteaching" activities. Ms. Adrian does not have to create this activity—merely select it. She will then provide a brief set of directions for that assignment as well as any necessary materials to the Omega Group. For the directions, she may merely copy an activity out of the math text with instructions along the lines of the following:

This activity requires some floor space (15′ by 15′), and a roll of masking tape. Students will place masking tape on the floor to develop an outline for a frequency table. The rows will represent choices of students' favorite singers (teachers should select five specific pictures of individual singers of different styles of music in advance from various popular music magazines). One column will be used for a count of individuals who like a particular singer, and another column will be used to write the digit of the number of persons who like a particular singer.

Based on a set of instructions such as this, the students in the Omega Group should be provided with a roll of masking tape, and then should do this activity in one corner of the room.

Given that the next direct instruction phase—the teacher directed phase—typically takes approximately 15 minutes, the group activity for Omega Group should be planned with that time frame in mind. Also, teachers should select an alternative activity that involves one or more of the multiple intelligences that have not been involved in the lesson. For example, in the activity above, the Omega Group is instructed to use masking tape and structure a "frequency table" on the floor. This grid will consist of a series of boxes in which students may stand as their preferences are noted. The Omega Group students would have to jointly plan what the tally table should look like, how big the boxes are going to be in order to hold various groups of students, and how the categories in the tally table should be organized.

In this activity, the box on the left is the "category" box, where pictures of singers may be placed in order to identify the specific category. That box need be only large enough to accommodate the pictures. In contrast, the box in the middle must be large enough for a number of students to stand in, as they stand by their preferences. The box on the right end will hold only a digit that summarizes the data in the middle box, so it can be somewhat smaller. The point is that the Omega Group has to figure all of this out—including the number of categories and the relative size of the boxes—while working as a group. The group then needs to place these boxes on the floor using the masking tape, for subsequent classroom use. Thus, this involves a variety of intelligences, including interpersonal intelligence, spatial intelligence, logical/mathematical intelligence, and bodily/kinesthetic intelligence.

Given the considerations in designing this floor grid, it is possible for the Omega Group to make a mistake in their work. For example, while the Omega Group may develop a five-by-three grid, they may forget to consider the relative size of the boxes. Specifically, rather than merely a set of tally marks—as in the earlier example on the dry erase board—the grid on the floor must include a second column of boxes that are large enough to hold a number of students. Thus, the challenge of making this grid is a more complicated activity than the example in the lesson orientation. This activity, while focusing on the lesson of data aggregation, is more intellectually demanding than the lesson activities offered to the mainline instructional group. Such tiering of instruction is characteristic of differentiated lessons.

THE MAINLINE INSTRUCTION GROUP

It is relatively easy in this classroom scenario to note the differentiation of lesson demands. After only a two- or three-minute orientation to the lesson and prior to having "taught" the lesson, Ms. Adrian has two groups of students in her class—the Omega Group and the mainline group (i.e., the group of students who were not torn out for the differentiated activity). As the Omega Group does its work, Ms. Adrian will engage in traditional teacher led initial instruction as she normally would for the mainline students. She may use a variety of activities from the instructor's manual, but she should make certain that a variety of activities are offered, and that her instruction addresses a variety of intelligences. For example, after she models how to formulate a tally table to summarize data, and transfers those data into a frequency table, she may have students work as peer buddies to do another sample problem on data aggregation and then explain their solution of the second problem to the mainline group within the class.

In order to further understand differentiated lesson planning, we should also consider what Ms. Adrian's teaching may look like. In a math class of 22 students, if she selected five students for the Omega Group, only 17 students would remain in the mainline group during the initial instruction, and they would be more homogeneously grouped. Consequently, Ms. Adrian's instruction is likely to improve. Consider the following questions:

1. Is it possible that Ms. Adrian's teaching is more focused for this mainline group?

2. Is Ms. Adrian less distracted by the gifted or advanced students who would be bored had they remained in the mainline group?

3. Is Ms. Adrian more likely to make eye contact more frequently with 17 students as compared with 22 students? Is Ms. Adrian likely to have a better sense of the level of understanding of this reduced number of students?

4. Are Ms. Adrian's examples during this teaching phase more likely to be on target for these students than if she were still working with the entire class?

Based on these questions, it seems reasonable to conclude that Ms. Adrian's instruction has become more focused and responsive to students' needs in this differentiated lesson given that she is working with a smaller group of students who need her assistance. This is the strength of differentiated instruction—it is strategically targeted instruction aimed at the learning needs of individual students in the math class.

THE BETA GROUP

After 15 minutes or so, Ms. Adrian will have completed the lesson orientation and the initial instructional phases for the mainline students. Also, the Omega Group will have completed its work in designing the grid on the floor. Again, the teacher should use the Guess, Assess, and Tear Out Tactic. With a few judicious questions, the teacher can again identify a second group of perhaps five or six other students in the mainline group who now understand the data aggregation concept and do not need the next direct instruction phase of teacher guided practice. We'll call this group the Beta Group. Again, Ms. Adrian would select this group from the mainline instructional group and provide an alternative assignment.

For example, this group may be provided the assignment to work with the Omega Group to "test out" the large frequency table grid that has been developed. The Beta Group could be given two or three frequency table assignments based on student preferences for (1) colors of tennis shoes worn in the class, (2) favorite musician, or (3) favorite national leader.

Of course at this point in the lesson, the Omega Group will also need another assignment. It would be perfectly appropriate to use them to work with the Beta Group to develop these activities for later classroom use. However, Ms. Adrian may wish to give them a separate assignment that involves writing several data aggregation problems for subsequent classroom use.

Again, we should consider what is happening in Ms. Adrian's class at this point in the lesson. First, note that Ms. Adrian's class will be quite differentiated only 15 minutes or so into the day's lesson. Specifically, after she oriented the students to the lesson, she tore out the Omega Group, and after the initial instruction phase, she tore out the Beta Group. Thus, after 15 minutes or so, five students in the Omega Group will be doing a second tear out assignment, the Beta Group will be testing the grid on the floor with several sample problems, and the mainline instructional group will include only 11 students who are receiving direct instruction from Ms. Adrian. Again, Ms. Adrian's instruction will be increasingly focused on these students in the mainline group who have not yet grasped the idea, and these students in turn will get the additional attention that they need from the teacher. Thus, differentiated instruction is very effective, strategically targeted teaching.

IDEAS FROM TEACHERS

Operations With Positive/Negative Integers

One interesting tiered instructional idea is to use the tear out group to create a rhythm, song, rhyme, or chant that can be used to teach some of the concepts in the lesson. This couples the use of musical intelligence with the need for differentiated group work. One teacher reported that her students created a nice little song to guide them in addition of positive and negative integers. This is sung to the tune of "Row, Row, Row Your Boat":

Same sign, add and keep,

Different sign subtract!

Take the sign of the highest number

Then you'll be exact!

IS FURTHER DIFFERENTIATION NEEDED?

It is difficult to address the question concerning how much differentiation is needed in any specific class or during any specific lesson. There is no obvious rule for how many different groups should be formed in any class for any particular lesson, but there are several points we can consider that teachers may use as guidelines. First, as shown in the Guess, Assess, and Tear Out chart presented previously, the differentiated lesson format requires that a teacher tear out a separate instructional group after each instructional phase. Thus, differentiated groups would be formed after the orientation to the lesson, after the initial instruction phase, after the teacher guided practice phase, and so forth.

The second point involves not overdoing it! To be specific, at some point in every lesson, this process of continual group formation breaks down. For example, after the teacher completed the initial instruction and tore out the Beta Group, he or she would be working with a mainline group of students who have not grasped the concept after the initial instructional phase. According to the direct instructional model, these students would move into teacher guided practice. However, if the students still do not have the basic concept at that point, why would any teacher force them to move into the next instructional phase? In fact, for students who do not grasp a concept after initial instruction, the teacher should move directly to the "reteach" phase and present the concept in a different way. Thus, at this point, the direct instructional phases have broken down and become nonapplicable.

Also, we must realize that there may be some confusion among some of the members of the Omega and Beta Groups. It is possible that some of those students, while believing that they understood the concept, did not have an adequate grasp of the idea after all. Thus, some of those students may need to rejoin the mainline instructional group. In fact, in a differentiated class, the instructional groups are quite fluid in the sense that they frequently change. Teachers should never be reluctant to tear out groups for brief specific activities or to re-include those same students in the mainline instruction should that become necessary.

Again, after the first two or three phases of instruction, the traditional direct instruction structure of the lesson breaks down. Further, by using differentiated groups the teacher is providing more focused learning and also will typically have a better grasp of where the students are in their learning. At that point, the original direct instructional model has become irrelevant for instructional purposes, since teachers will have various groups of kids at various phases of learning. This fluid differentiation is the very substance of a differentiated lesson.

ANYTHING WRONG WITH THIS SCENARIO? ENHANCING THE DIFFERENTIATED INSTRUCTION MODEL

Have you noticed several problems in the scenario noted earlier? I have learned, in workshops around the country, to initially describe the process as I first conceived it, and then to highlight several misconceptions on my part within the teaching scenario just presented. After numerous workshops on this topic, I am confident that this is a more effective teaching procedure than merely describing the total process. Thus, as a cognitive challenge, can you find the several errors that I have made? Do you see several problems in the scenario as it is described up to this point? As a guide, consider the following questions:

1. Have we used the best instructional techniques for the students who need them least?

2. Using this plan, are we using students to teach other students? Are we sure that the first group of students understands the concept?

3. Are we always tearing out the "best and brightest"?

4. Are we providing the most effective instruction to everyone?

5. Are various multiple intelligences employed in learning?

As these questions show, my first conceptualization of the Guess, Assess, and Tear Out Tactic was not completely thought out. Given the scenario, the teacher will always identify the best and brightest for the first tear out groups. Also, in the scenario, the most effective instruction—the movement-based grid development activity—is presented to the students who need that instruction least. For these reasons, we'll need to modify the scenario above a bit to see its true beauty and realize the overall efficacy of differentiated instruction.

> For tiered activities, teachers should not always tear out the same group of students after the orientation to the lesson, as this would result in the same students—the best and the brightest—always working together and always working independently of direct teacher supervision.

Rather, to form that first tear out group—the Omega Group—the teacher should identify two or three students who have firmly grasped the concept and partner them with several students who have not. This type of heterogeneous grouping will involve many more students than in the scenario I have described. Also, such heterogeneous groups are more likely to result in student-to-student learning during the activities of the Omega Group as those students work together independently of the teacher. For example, if students working in one of the tear out groups have questions, they should be told to ask those questions first of the other group members. In that fashion, students can, and should, be learning from each other much more frequently in schools than is common in the traditional class. In this way, the differentiated instructional concept provides one alternative to facilitate such student-to-student learning. Thus, one fundamental rule in the formulation of every tear out group is to select some students who have grasped the concept and some who haven't.

Another problem can be noted in the scenario: With the Omega group doing the instructional design of the grid on the floor, the students in the mainline group will be likely to pay attention to that group rather than to the traditional instruction being offered to the mainline students. In order to offset this problem, Ms. Adrian must make the instruction offered to the mainline group every bit as interesting, as novel, and as much fun as any of the alternative assignments offered to the tear out groups. In the scenario above, once the Omega Group is identified and given their assignment of making a grid in one corner of the classroom (which is a highly active, movement-based learning opportunity), the teacher should take the students in the mainline group to another corner of the classroom and present them with a highly active, movement-based task. In fact, it is perfectly acceptable to use the same activity. The only difference will be that the students in the mainline group will be more closely supervised by Ms. Adrian. The point is that once teachers begin to offer novel, exciting, activity-based learning in their classes, they will find it necessary to offer such activities to all students. Again, this is one of the strengths of differentiated instruction.

GUIDELINES FOR DIFFERENTIATED LESSON PLANNING

With these several modifications in mind, we can now identify the general guidelines for modifying a direct instructional lesson and transforming it into a differentiated lesson in math. I do wish to emphasize that these are merely guidelines, and that every teacher should, based on his or her understanding of the individuals in the class as well as the demands of the subject content, adapt these to the specific needs of the students. These guidelines are presented below.

TEACHING TACTICS

GUIDELINES FOR DIFFERENTIATED INSTRUCTION LESSONS

1. Subdivide the class early and often. The teacher in a differentiated class should provide many tear out activities. In fact, teachers employing differentiated instruction will subdivide their class much earlier in the lesson than is usual in the direct instruction model, and will do so much more frequently. For this reason, the Guess, Assess, and Tear Out Tactic offers the most effective, differentiated instructional option for students at all levels of ability in the class. When teaching within a differentiated instructional lesson, teachers should tear out a heterogeneous group of students for an alternative instructional activity after each phase in the traditional lesson plan. Teachers should select some students who have grasped the concept and some who haven't, by exercising judgment concerning who can work effectively in a group and who can or will work together.

2. Never plan just one activity when you need two or three! The academic diversity in today's elementary classes often necessitates the presentation of the same content in multiple ways, so I suggest that each time a teacher plans one activity, he or she plans at least one more and subdivides the class, with some students doing one and some doing the other. While creative teachers can always generate interesting instructional ideas, many ideas can be found in today's teachers' manuals for math curricula. These are typically included as "enrichment" or "alternative teaching" ideas. In most cases, teachers merely need to select these activities from the curriculum ideas presented.

3. Use the tear out activities more than once in the unit. In the example in Ms. Adrian's class, the Omega group was the first to develop a frequency table on the floor. On subsequent days within that unit of instruction, other students in other groups may also be challenged with that activity. Further, it is perfectly acceptable for a particular student to be included in several groups doing the same activity. That would merely be a good example of a repetitive instructional technique!

4. Modify alternative activities to address different multiple intelligences. Ms. Adrian, in using the grid activity in her class, provided an activity that emphasized several intelligences, including spatial, logical/mathematical, and interpersonal. Can this activity be modified and subsequently used to involve other intelligences? If the assignment were to blindfold a student, and have him or her provide verbal directions for the formulation of the grid on the floor without watching the process, could linguistic intelligence be strengthened?

5. Use what you have in the local community! In math instruction, as well as many other subjects, using examples in the students' community can involve students more and motivate them to complete the math. For example, in farming communities, tying math problems to local crop sales can be quite effective. For students in urban areas, describing math problems in terms of the types of clothes or tennis shoes that are in vogue can motivate students more than simply using whatever math problems are on the page. If students live near a major historical park, teachers should consider math examples that could be tied to that local resource (e.g., How many patriots fought at the Battle of Trenton versus how many British mercenaries?).

Teachers in every field should use examples from the community whenever possible. One interesting type of assignment for some tear out groups is to rewrite each of the word problems in a particular unit using some local example. The others in the class can then use those problems for their practice work. This results in more "authentic" learning than some of the math problems presented in the standard math texts.

6. Tie students in emotionally. We now know that, prior to learning, the student must sense emotional safety in the learning environment. Further, if teachers can tie the math content to an emotional hook, students will become more involved in the content. Discussions of math in terms of the number of students who can go on a school trip might be one illustration of this idea. Here are two more examples:

Grade 3 Problem: "We have 4 buses for the third-grade trip, and each will carry 25 students and 4 supervisory adults. If 22 adults volunteer to go on the trip, how many students can go?"

Grade 6 Problem: "We have 4 buses, each of which will take 25 students and 4 adults. If students were selected for the class trip based on their math grades, and 80% of a total student math population of 112 students scored high enough to go, would we have to leave eligible students or adult volunteers behind?"

If students have parents in the military, a number of math problems on various troop strengths can be used. I noted this personally while working in the schools in Clarkesville, Tennessee, since that city is adjacent to the military base that houses the 101st Airborne Division—a division that had recently been deployed overseas.

(Continued)

(Continued)

7. Use differentiated instruction for inclusive classes. While including students with significant disabilities in general education math classes is not new, the use of differentiated instruction as a basis for inclusion is. The overall fit between inclusion and differentiated instruction is almost perfect; again we seem to owe another tribute to Carol Tomlinson, PhD, for her groundbreaking work on this concept. Teachers should jointly plan to use differentiated lessons in inclusion classes. Moreover, with both a general educator and a special educator in the class, the monitoring of the tear out groups is much more easily managed!

8. Continue some traditional lessons. I encourage teachers not to attempt differentiated lessons each and every day. While lectures seem ineffective with many students today, other aspects of traditional instruction work wonderfully, including group project activities, whole class discussions of video- or media-based examples, student presentations, and independent student research. These instructional activities should always be an important component of learning in the elementary classroom.

One question I am frequently asked is, How often should teachers differentiate? I usually tell teachers to aim for a highly differentiated lesson structure perhaps three days each week, and on the alternate days utilize more traditional instructional procedures, such as those mentioned above. I believe that this will provide an appropriate mix of activities and will create an effective classroom learning environment where the needs of all students can be met. I also find that teachers respond to this suggestion positively; while teachers have a difficult time seeing themselves teaching three or four groups of students in different tasks during each 15-minute segment each day of the week, they can see themselves doing this two or three days each week and using other effective whole group tactics on the other days.

9. Teachers should "test the waters" of differentiated instruction tentatively. Once a teacher decides to attempt differentiated instruction, he or she should try this approach in a successful class—a classroom that seems to be working well. The teacher should also initially do this in an area of math that students know well. This will effectively increase the teacher's comfort zone, and will be more likely to result in a pleasant teaching experience, than trying this new teaching paradigm in a challenging class. Also, testing this idea in a class that is not presenting challenges is more likely to result in initial success. After that, teachers can expand into other, more challenging classes. Moreover, teachers who have moved into this slowly and have seen it work as both they and the students grow to understand this instructional system, have stated that teaching is simply much more fun this way!

RESULTS OF DIFFERENTIATED LESSONS

Teachers who have chosen to move into differentiation for instruction in math have generally found that many of the anxieties they had about such instruction did not materialize. For example, many teachers are initially concerned about the issue of management of varied groups within the classroom. Of course, every class includes some students who, at least initially, should not be selected for tear out activities since their behavior patterns necessitate close teacher supervision. However, teachers typically find that after the class as a whole gets accustomed to this learning format, even those behaviorally challenged kids can participate meaningfully in tear out activities.

Also, because the training of most teachers in schools today was formulated on the direct instruction model, some teachers cannot bring themselves to believe that learning will take place in the tear out groups; some teachers view these unsupervised groups as disasters waiting to happen. Nevertheless, I've had teachers state repeatedly that once they moved to a differentiated instruction format, they found that students do learn from each other in the tear out groups, and that this instructional format results in increased student learning overall. All teachers are under pressure today to address the math standards mandated by every state department of education; this learning format will result in improved instruction compared to whole class, traditional instruction. Teachers, however, must exercise some judgment in initial group formulation.

The chart below lists the typical results reported by teachers once they begin the transition to a truly differentiated classroom.

Results of Guess, Assess, and Tear Out

1. *Provision of Varied Instruction.* This offers the most effective instructional option for all students in today's classes.

2. *Increased Involvement of Advanced Students.* The advanced kids in this procedure will be more challenged and thus less likely to get bored and engage in problem behaviors.

3. *Varied Behavior Management Concerns.* Management of an increased number of instructional groups will be a concern, and the teacher should move into differentiation slowly for this reason. Students who would otherwise be bored with traditional lessons will be more engaged in this instructional model, however, and it is hoped these behavior management results will effectively even things out for the teacher in the differentiated lesson.

4. *Improved Instruction for Those Who Need It.* As the mainline group gets smaller the instruction for that group is likely to improve, since the teacher is concentrating on a smaller group. Thus, the teacher is providing increased support for the students who really need the help on a particular lesson.

5. *Provision of the Best Instruction for Everyone.* Differentiated instruction encourages teachers to offer the most effective enrichment/instruction to kids across the ability spectrum. Teachers must make the mainline group activities as varied, as novel, and as exciting as any of the alternative assignments for the tear out groups.

6. *Effective Use as a Model for Inclusive Instruction.* Teachers can readily see the comfortable fit between the use of multiple tear out groups, formed to be

heterogeneous, and the demands of the inclusive classroom. Differentiated instruction provides one of the most effective models for inclusion currently available.

7. *Teachers Become Used to Teaching This Way.* Once teachers try this instructional model, particularly if they test this model in an academic area within their comfort zone, they typically find that they enjoy this type of teaching. While all teachers differentiate to some degree, teachers who devote themselves to this approach often state that they would not like to return to teaching in a traditional fashion. In fact, teaching a differentiated lesson is simply more fun.

A DIFFERENTIATED INSTRUCTION OVERVIEW: WHAT IT IS AND WHAT IT ISN'T

With the guidelines for differentiation of instruction in mind, we can now take a broader look at the overall concept. When I first began to investigate differentiated instruction, I was somewhat confused as to what it really was. I have since learned that such confusion is quite common. Specifically, in many books I read and in many workshops I attended I found that a wide variety of great teaching ideas were presented, but I found no "central theme" on what differentiated instruction was. While I always enjoy acquiring novel teaching ideas, I left many such workshops wondering if "differentiated instruction" was merely an array of "good teaching ideas." I had not grasped the essential element or elements of the concept.

More recently, I have come to understand that differentiation is more than merely an innovative set of novel teaching tactics. Differentiated instruction is, in reality, a new way of conceptualizing learning in the classroom context. Teachers in the 21st century should no longer believe that children make up a "class" of third graders or a "class" of sixth graders.

> Rather than teachers considering students as a "class," differentiated instruction requires that they plan lessons, generate activities, and conduct assessments based on the needs of individual children rather than on groups of children who happen to be the same chronological age.

Again, differentiated instruction represents a real paradigm shift for teachers who have been trained to think of instruction as a group phenomenon—as in the direct instructional model described earlier.

Teachers must now shift their thinking to lesson planning for individual children, and they must consider the emerging information on the wide variety of ways that children learn (e.g., multiple intelligences, peer learning, etc.). Only from such a perspective can teachers hope to meet the wide variety of needs in today's classrooms.

I have further come to realize that many teachers are differentiating their math classes without realizing it. Indeed, many teachers have been "differentiating" their classrooms for many years. The academic diversity found in today's classes would suggest that in order to survive as teachers, we must be about the business of novel and innovative teaching to diverse groups of students within the class. For these math teachers, the construct of the differentiated lesson plan will merely mean that they develop their different instructional activities more deliberately, more strategically. These teachers will then deliver a more diversified lesson within the math class, having initially planned to address these diverse learning needs.

WHAT'S NEXT?

At this point, we have investigated the brain research as well as the practical concerns in formulating a differentiated lesson in math. The next chapter presents techniques that will assist in learning early math skills in kindergarten and the lower grades. In the next chapter, and all subsequent chapters, a variety of instructional ideas is presented, but these must be placed in the context of a strategically developed differentiated lesson plan, as described in this chapter.

Differentiating for Abstract Math Comprehension

3

STEPS IN DEVELOPING EARLY MATH SKILLS

A number of researchers have considered how students master early math skills, and the common element, appearing repeatedly in the teaching guidelines, is the "concreteness" necessary for early math instruction (Fuson & Wearne, 1997; Gurganus, 2004; Jordan, Miller, & Mercer, 1998). Chapter 1 presented a number of guidelines for the development of number sense, and many of these ideas involved very concrete examples of mathematical algorithms. Further, the mastery of early math skills beyond the number sense level also involves use of concrete objects, representational instruction in which pictures of objects are used as teaching tools, or both. Of course, for students throughout the elementary grades who may be struggling and thus several years behind in mathematics achievement, concreteness is no less important than in kindergarten and the early grades.

In addition to the need for concrete instruction, teachers must understand the various levels of skill development in early math. Fuson and Wearne (1997) developed a sequence of early math skills that many teachers find helpful in considering how young brains learn math beyond the number sense level. These researchers postulated that children learn their numbers in a pattern—consistent with the emerging brain research suggesting that all brains search for patterns. Fuson and Wearne (1997) attempted to identify the patterns in early math, and subsequently identified five different stages of early learning. The stages are referred to as the UDSSI model (see below). Each letter represents a stage of learning, and Fuson and Wearne (1997) suggest that children must learn each step in sequence in order to understand multidigit numbers and higher math problems. The stages are presented below.

Stages of the UDSSI Model of Early Math Skills

The Unitary Stage

This represents the early understanding of numerals and the numbers they represent. Children initially learn that ten means "ten objects." Knowing the order of the numbers one through nine allows young children to understand numbers, and their early understanding of the concept of place value allows students to understand numbers up to the early teens. Thus, children in the unitary stage comprehend the numbers one through 19 fairly well.

The Decade Stage

This stage involves children's understanding the concept of counting by tens, as well as numbers higher than 19. Many children comprehend the order of 21, 22, 23, or 35, 36, and 37, et cetera, but they do not know the order of the numbers in the tens place for subsequent groups of ten (e.g., is 32 higher than 51?). These children may count up through the 20s and then go to the 50s. Children who understand the decades know the order of the numbers in the tens place (i.e., the decades). Children who understand the decades can count from one through 99.

The Sequence Stage

This involves children beginning to understand the sequence of tens and ones. Children learn that 53 means five tens and three ones. They realize that when a person states a number, the first part is written first and the last part is written second (i.e., 53 is written by writing a 5 and then a 3, in that order). These children are then able to write the numbers in order. Prior to this understanding, children may write 53 as 50 and 3 and then combine these as 503.

The Separate Stage

This involves children realizing that the numbers mean something even though such meaning is not stated. Children at this stage understand that even though "ten" is not stated in the number 55, the first digit really means five tens and the second digit means five ones. Children who comprehend this step can separate the tens and ones.

The Integrated Stage

This stage begins when children begin to combine the sequence and separate stages. Students who understand numbers at this stage have flexibility in approaching and solving problems using two-digit numbers because they can rapidly shift attributes of the "10s" in the tens place to either the background or foreground in their thinking. They also understand that the order of one through nine is repeated throughout the hundreds, thousands, and so forth.

With this model in mind, we can understand how students learn early addition. According to this model, children learn addition and subtraction of single digit numbers in three levels, as shown below (Fuson & Wearne, 1997).

Level 1: Children at this level use objects as a model for addition or subtraction. Children move the objects to solve the problems, and thus are using a very concrete learning method. The objects may either be part of the total or part of the addend, but the objects are essential at this level.

Level 2: Children at this level use the "count on" method by counting onto the addend, and in using this method do not need the concrete objects in order to solve the problem. This is based, in part, on growing memory skills, since children at this level are capable of keeping track of the amount represented by the first addend as well as the second addend.

Level 3: Children at this level can "chunk" the information together to get a total. These children can look at the problem and chunk (i.e., mentally regroup the numbers), which allows fairly easy calculation of the answer. This is the highest level of early addition skill. These students no longer need models or the "counting on" method to reach the solution, but are able to get to the total by grouping and chunking known facts.

Fuson and Wearne (1997) also suggested that these levels may apply to mathematics understanding at a higher level. For example, children solving two-digit addition and subtraction problems go through basically the same steps as above. Children at Level 1 use a model by placing the first number of objects and either adding or subtracting the next number and then counting the total to reach the solution. Children at Level 2 tend to use mental markers to get the total. These children remember where they start and either "count up" or "take away" to get the answers. Children at Level 3 can chunk information to get the total.

Using this model can benefit teachers in almost all the elementary grades with students who are challenged by early operations; they can better understand exactly where a child's mathematical strengths are. Further, this construct provides a solid theoretical basis for the use of manipulatives or concrete examples across the elementary grades for students struggling in math.

Web Site Review: Basic Math Facts

The Math Fact Café Web site provides teachers with a tool to set up a math facts activity on the computer involving facts for Grades K through 3. This can be a quick, free way to generate computer assisted activities that are specific to individual sets of math facts (e.g., three's times tables, or math fact division by 6). Typically these activities involve presentation of

(Continued)

(Continued)

20 math facts, one at a time, with the opportunity for the student to type in his or her answer and check the accuracy of that answer. The software keeps a running tally of the percentage of corrects and errors, and after 20 problems are completed, the screen shows each problem with the incorrect problems corrected and highlighted. Graphics are not included, and the reward for a correct answer is presentation of a term such as *Awesome*; problems answered incorrectly result in presentation of terms such as *Bummer*. In general, for today's software this provides minimal stimulation for either corrects or errors, and this presentation may result in students being less than motivated to do this activity after the first few times. Still, this is one option for quick presentation of computerized math facts.

www.mathfactcafe.com

TEACHING STRATEGY: A CONCRETE, SEMI-CONCRETE, ABSTRACT LEARNING TACTIC

Students master early math beyond the number sense level most effectively when instruction is presented in concrete, semi-concrete, and abstract ways; such a three-level presentation is referred to as CSA (Allsopp, 1999; Jordan, Miller, & Mercer, 1998). This approach is also occasionally referred to as CRA, with the letters spelling out concrete, representational, and abstract. This instructional method has been shown to be highly effective, but it is still not in widespread use in many classrooms beyond the first few grades. Brain research, however, has documented that information presented in a variety of different ways is much more likely to be retained over a longer period of time (Sousa, 2001). Thus, CSA is now recommended for use in general education classrooms throughout the elementary grades to help all students successfully learn difficult math concepts (Harris, Miller, & Mercer, 1995; Marsh & Cooke, 1996). Further, research has shown that this approach should be used more frequently even in high school for students who are struggling in math.

What Is CSA?

Almost all educators would agree that abstract learning is the most efficient means of problem solving in math at any grade level, because concrete or semi-concrete examples can get quite cumbersome for higher level mathematics. Yet for many students across the elementary years, concrete or semi-concrete learning may be necessary during the initial instruction in a particular math concept. In the differentiated classroom, providing tear out group work using concrete or semi-concrete examples is one way to offer varied instruction and meet the needs of all students. Further, with the emphasis on inclusion of students with special needs in the general education classroom setting, teachers will out of necessity begin to use CSA methods to teach math skills in the differentiated math class, because many students with disabilities will require this type of instruction.

Shaw-Jing, Stigler, and Woodward (2000) refer to CSA as the "mental tool" view of math instruction, which suggests that mental images of mathematic equations or problems may best be formed using physical materials or concrete objects. You will recall from Chapter 1 that visual processing is highly involved in mathematical thinking (Sousa, 2001), suggesting that students need to "visualize" math problems in order to understand them. Clearly, concrete objects or pictorial representations of them can greatly assist in this visualization process. These mental tools are then used to guide the students in their problem solving. The mental tool view uses highly organized and structured representations of the numbers. This view suggests that if the representation is highly structured, it will provide the student with a tool that can assist in visualization of the math problem.

> In short, learning to use concrete objects and semi-concrete representations is a prerequisite to abstract learning for many students; and for students who struggle in math, use of CSA instructional approaches can be critical.

While the use of CSA has received a boost from recent brain research and the current emphasis on differentiation of math activities, Shaw-Jing and colleagues (2000) point out that this instructional paradigm is not new. Many years ago, Stern (1949) developed a pattern that used a wooden stick with groves to slide into wooden blocks. Ten sticks would go in each wooden block, and students would use these counters to assist in problem solving. Others subsequently developed a variety of grids or counting devices to reflect the base-ten number system. Thus, concrete and semi-concrete models have thus been employed in math for a long time; there are many variations on this older instructional approach.

IDEAS FROM TEACHERS

Counting Money: Coins With Stickers!

One CSA technique that has been around for many years is the use of coins to teach counting change. Here are a couple of new and interesting variations on that theme. In counting change, students must be proficient at counting by fives, and many students are not. Thus, teachers may place stickers on the coins themselves to represent their value. Place a white sticker with a "1" written on it on the nickels, a sticker with a "2" on the dimes, and a sticker with a "5" written on it on the quarters. Next, you should model for the students how to count change using this system. When presented with a pile of coins, students should separate them and begin counting with the large coins first (the coins with the highest number on the sticker—not the physically largest of the coins). Students are told to count by fives as many times as the coin's sticker indicates (e.g., for a quarter they would count by fives, five times, saying "five, ten, fifteen, twenty, twenty-five"). Next the students should be told to remember that amount, and then move to the next largest of the coins, and "count on," beginning with the first amount. Again they count by fives for as many times as that coin says. When they are finished with the quarter, dimes, and nickels, all they have to do is count by ones for the pennies. Often, students who seem unable to learn to count change in any other fashion can suddenly count by fives to reach the correct sum. After the students are proficient in the strategy, the teacher should slowly phase out the use of stickers.

Hairy Coins!

As another interesting variation on this theme, teachers can use "hairy money." Rather than stickers with numbers written on them, teachers may tape short hairs (perhaps using yarn if hair is not available) to large pictures of the coins on the dry erase board. The picture of a quarter would have five hairs on it, a dime two hairs, and a nickel one hair. Pennies have no hairs and are counted by counting ones.

Clearly, because of brain-compatible research as well as the necessity to differentiate instruction in the inclusive class, the CSA approach has been revitalized. Further, the current recommendations from the research suggest that application of this approach for higher level learners will be quite useful. To get both younger and older students who may be having difficulty in math used to using concrete or semi-concrete mathematical representations, Shaw-Jing et al. (2000) developed a set of game-like activities, as presented below. To make many of these games a "peer buddy" activity, pairs of students can merely use a spinner, rather than have the teacher call out numbers or patterns, as in the description below.

TEACHING TACTICS

GAMES FOR TEACHING REPRESENTATIONAL MATH

1. Pattern Number Bingo. This uses a standard Bingo-style board with pictures in patterned sets on it. These may be tally marks in groups of five; thus "7" would be represented as ///// //. The board should include patterns representing numbers one through ten. Teachers hold up a pattern card, and students place a marker on their Bingo card if that pattern is present. This game is meant to help students learn to enumerate and associate numerals with patterns.

2. Memory Cards. This game uses two different color decks of cards. One deck of cards had the numerals 0–10 on it. The other deck of cards has groups of objects representing zero through ten on them. The students turn one card from each color deck over. If the cards represent the same number, the student collects the cards and goes again. This game is intended to motivate students to memorize the representational patterns for the numerals.

3. Flash Pattern Cards. This game assists students in quickly recognizing patterns for numerals. Children have to quickly find a correct numeral card for a pattern card flashed by the teacher for three to five seconds. The students will enjoy seeing how fast they can find the card matching the number pattern presented by the teacher.

4. The Relay Race. This game is similar to hop scotch. Students line up in front of a number grid that is pre-drawn on the floor. Students draw pattern cards from a bag, decipher the pattern, and stand on the correlating number on the grid. The students can use this idea to work on numeration and number sets. This movement activity makes mathematics fun and incorporates movement into learning, as recommended by the brain-compatible research discussed previously.

5. How Many Do You See? In this game students are shown a numeral on a big picture card. The students then create a pattern to correspond to the numeral, using pictures of any object they wish. The group may then be asked questions about the pattern made. For example, a student who used pictures of human "stick men" to represent the numeral five might be asked how many legs the stick figures had altogether. This game assists in relating mathematics to the real world.

6. Addition Quizmo. This game has several steps. First, the teacher calls out a number between zero and five. The students place that many markers (use any type of concrete counters here) on a Bingo card. Then the teacher calls out another number and the students next place that many additional markers on the paper. The students then look on their Bingo cards for the total number represented by the markers, and place a marker over that number on the Bingo card if they find a match. Teachers may have the students explain their answers.

7. The Difference War. This game is the same as Addition Quizmo, but the students practice subtraction (referred to as "take away"). The Bingo cards and the markers are used for subtraction in the same fashion as in Addition Quizmo above.

8. Start From Five. This game is a combination of Addition Quizmo and The Difference War. The teacher always starts with a 5, and presents addition or subtraction problems (e.g., $5 + 4 =$ _____, or $5 - 2 =$ _____). If the student's Bingo card has a match to the sum or the difference required, the student places a marker on the Bingo card.

9. Make Ten. This game uses a deck of cards for each student and a target card deck used by the teacher. A target card is flipped over. The students then turn over a card from their deck. If the sum adds up to 10 (i.e., Make Ten), then the student moves the card off to the side. If the turned card does not make ten, then the card is placed back into the deck. The student who gets rid of his or her deck of cards first wins.

Research has strongly supported the use of CSA for students across the elementary grades (Allsopp, 1999; Harris, Miller, & Mercer, 1995; Jordan, Miller, & Mercer, 1998). A recent study by Jordan and colleagues (1998) used the CSA method to teach three groups of students in a fourth-grade inclusive general education class. The study included 125 students, some with learning disabilities, some average students, and some gifted students, in teaching a lesson on fractions. The results demonstrated that CSA produced significantly better learning and maintenance for *all students* than the traditional textbook-based instructional method. This study found that the CSA method was effective in teaching students fraction identification, comparison, equivalence, and computation using fractions. Further, the students also maintained these new skills in posttests one and two weeks after the end of instruction. These results suggest that CSA can be used successfully in the general education classroom to help all students, including students with math learning problems, successfully learn difficult math concepts.

The study described above is critical because of its demonstration of the efficacy of CSA for students with learning disabilities. Students with learning disabilities, the single largest group of students with disabilities, are also the students most likely to be included in the general education math curriculum. Thus, in the differentiated math class, teachers must find ways to include these students in the activities. Yet these students often struggle with math, and many display certain learning characteristics that amplify difficulties in various areas of math. For example, many students with learning disabilities exhibit visual and auditory perception problems that negatively affect mastery of math. In general, students with learning disabilities will also have trouble reading the math problems or using highly specialized mathematics language such as the *language* of fractions (i.e., with terms such as *numerator, denominator, mixed numbers,* and *tenths*). The use of CSA can foster efficient learning of math concepts and provide these learners with strategies to solve problems in every math area.

USING CSA IN THE CLASSROOM

CSA incorporates three cognitive levels of explicit instruction in math skills (Allsopp, 1999). The first level, representing the lowest level of comprehension, is the concrete level. This involves the use of manipulative objects during instruction, such as tally marks for numerals, circles divided into fractional parts, or even edibles such as an orange divided into its segments. The second level is the semi-concrete level, which uses representations of concrete objects in instruction, such as drawings of objects. The abstract instructional level uses no hands-on support materials.

In the concrete phase, teachers use manipulatives that can readily be configured to portray the concept being taught. These can be purchased (e.g., counters) or may be inexpensive, teacher-made materials. In this stage, the teacher would instruct students in how to manipulate the objects to simulate the math problem. Also, teachers should include worksheets for students to record results of problem solving. Most students in schools today are exposed to foam rubber sections of a "pie" and can recall examples of concrete instruction of this nature; in the lower grades this instruction is quite common.

In the semi-concrete phase teachers use visual representations of the manipulatives used during the concrete phase. Also, students are exposed to other, similar graphic representations on paper, as well as spaces to draw their own representations as needed. Semi-concrete representations are frequently used in teaching fractions, but these representations are not often used in the general education class beyond the lower grades for teaching other math skills such as whole number operations for large numbers and/or problem solving. For example, in one widely used math curriculum for elementary grades, I recently found the semi-concrete representations of operations to be quite common in the Grade 1 teacher's manual. These representations were still present in the Grade 3 teacher's manual. By Grade 5, however, such semi-concrete representations had disappeared from the teacher's manual altogether.

This represents a significant problem in most modern math curricula, because the semi-concrete phase can be critical for many students in the higher elementary and middle school grades who are experiencing difficulty in math. In the differentiated math class, teachers must make certain that they do not skip this stage simply because the curriculum materials may do so. Rather, teachers should develop and provide examples of all types of math problems in semi-concrete fashion. Further, each time a concrete or semi-concrete demonstration is given, the teacher (or another student) should verbally direct the other students through the concrete or semi-concrete example, stressing the relationship to the math concept under discussion. Thus, in presenting either concrete or semi-concrete instruction, the teacher will likewise be presenting abstract instruction.

Presented below are several examples of how numeric operations of higher level elementary math skills may be taught using semi-concrete representations. While most math texts today do not present a wide array of such examples, having one tear out group develop several problems with such representations is an excellent differentiation activity.

TEACHING TACTICS

SAMPLE SEMI-CONCRETE MATH PROBLEMS FOR ELEMENTARY GRADES

1. Jennie had $82 but she owed $31 to Jonathan. After paying that debt, how much did Jennie have left?

Jennie's Money	Money She Gave to Jonathan
$$$$$ $$$$$ $$$$$ $$$$$	$$$$$ $$$$$ $$$$$ $$$$$
$$$$$ $$$$$ $$$$$ $$$$$	$$$$$ $$$$$ $
$$$$$ $$$$$ $$$$$ $$$$$	
$$$$$ $$$$$ $$$$$ $$$$$	
$$	

$82   Minus $31   equals _____

To solve this problem, the students should draw a circle around the dollar signs in Jennie's money that are equivalent to the money she gave to Jonathan. They will then count the remaining funds, using the groups of fives.

2. Here is a sample of a regrouping problem for three-digit subtraction: $324 - 245 =$ _____?

///////// /////////	///////// /////////	///////// /////////	///////// /////////////
///////// /////////	///////// /////////	///////// /////////	
///////// /////////	///////// /////////	///////// /////////	
///////// /////////	///////// /////////	///////// /////////	
///////// /////////	///////// /////////	///////// /////////	

(Continued)

(Continued)

	3 100s	2 tens	4 ones
Minus	2 100s	4 tens	5 ones

////////// //////////   ////////// //////////   ////////// ////////// /////

////////// //////////   ////////// //////////   ////////// //////////

////////// //////////   ////////// //////////

////////// //////////   ////////// //////////

////////// //////////   ////////// //////////

Leaves	2 100s	4 tens	5 ones

Beginning with the digit on the left, the student must regroup the problem in the tens and ones places as follows:

3 100s and 2 tens and 4 ones =
2 100s and 11 tens and 14 ones

////////// //////////   ////////// //////////   ////////// ////////// //////////   ////////// ////

////////// //////////   ////////// //////////   ////////// //////////

////////// //////////   ////////// //////////   ////////// //////////

////////// //////////   ////////// //////////   ////////// //////////

////////// //////////   ////////// //////////   ////////// //////////

Next, the student will cross out the number of tally marks equal to the subtrahend and then calculate the remaining tally marks.

In the abstract phase, mathematics problems without any representations are used, but such worksheets also can be constructed to include space on the sheet for students to develop their own representation of the problem. Further, teachers should encourage students to do so, if such visualization and drawing helps students better understand the math problem. Again, all math curricula include abstract problems as the final assessment of skill mastery, and such abstract thinking should be the teacher's overall goal. However, many students need semi-concrete instruction in higher grade levels. Further, although many students do not do well in math across the grade levels, curriculum materials companies have continued to present abstract problems in the upper grades without appropriate representational examples. Thus, many teachers may be reluctant to include the semi-concrete problems described here beyond a certain grade level. Again, while CSA problems have always provided the basis for most math instruction in kindergarten and the lower grades, teachers should now employ concrete and semi-concrete instruction in higher grade levels throughout the elementary years. In fact, modern theorists are recommending that concrete and semi-concrete examples should be used throughout the grade levels, up to and including introductory algebra (Allsopp, 1999; Maccini, McNaughton, & Ruhl, 1999). In order to demonstrate this concept, the problem below provides an example of the CSA representation of higher order math, as recommended and described by Allsopp (1999).

TEACHING TACTICS

ALLSOPP'S CONCRETE ALGEBRAIC EXAMPLE

Imagine solving for "a" when teaching the algebraic equation 2a + 3a + 5 = 25.

This can be represented by physical objects as follows. A saucer or paper plate can represent "a"; thus two paper plates would represent "2a." Put two paper plates together on a desk. Cut a piece of tag board into strips that are one inch wide and three inches long. Use two of these to make a cross to represent the addition sign. Then place three plates in a group to represent "3a."

Next you will need some smaller counters (perhaps plastic counters) to illustrate the "+ 5" in the equation. Place two more strips to represent the second addition sign, and then place five counters to represent the "5." Finally, place two strips of tag board parallel to represent an equals sign. Your example would then look like this:

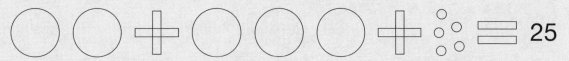

Next, you will need to introduce the concept of a balance beam to "balance" the equation in the middle. The equals sign represents the fulcrum, and your balance beam will look like this:

$$2a + 3a + 5 \qquad = \qquad 25$$
$$\overline{}$$
$$\Delta$$

When we take away five counters from one side, the beam is unbalanced, and will look like this:

$$2a + 3a$$
$$=$$
$$\Delta \qquad\qquad\qquad 25$$

We'll correct that by taking away five counters from the right side also, and then the beam will look like this:

$$2a + 3a \qquad = \qquad 20$$
$$\overline{}$$
$$\Delta$$

Next we'll add the 2a and the 3a to make 5a, but since we took nothing away, the beam is still balanced:

$$5a \qquad\qquad = \qquad 20$$
$$\overline{}$$
$$\Delta$$

Finally, we'll divide both sides by five to find the value of "a." Thus, the value of "a" is 4.

SUMMARY: CSA TACTIC

In differentiated classrooms, teachers need access to a wide variety of math strategies; the use of concrete or semi-concrete instruction can assist many students who are currently struggling in math. Moreover, CSA can provide a variety of tear out activities across the grade levels. As is apparent from the examples above, the semi-concrete or representational stage of learning is now being employed in much higher grades, and the research on the use of this tactic is strongly supportive (Allsopp, 1999; Harris, Miller, & Mercer, 1995; Jordan, Miller, & Mercer, 1998; Marsh & Cooke, 1996; Shaw-Jing et al., 2000). Clearly, teachers who wish to move into differentiated instruction should implement instruction using this CSA tactic.

IDEAS FROM TEACHERS

Using CSA

Multiplication Tables and Popsicle Sticks!

One teacher developed a great way to represent multiplication using Popsicle sticks to represent the lower times tables. For example, in teaching the three's times tables, students may use three sticks to make a triangle on their desk. Then they count the sides (which equal three). They should then say, "One triangle with three sides equals three Popsicle sticks" and then shorten that to "One times three equals three."

Next, they add another triangle and count all of the sides (which equal six). They would say, "Two triangles with three sides each equal six sticks" or "Two times three equals six." They continue this process until they have ten triangles on their desks, representing the entire times table.

The same activity can be repeated using squares to represent multiples of four and stars to represent fives and sixes. This activity involves many brain processes in the sense that students are manipulating objects, repeating verbal equations, and visually seeing the demonstration of the times tables. Thus, this activity would involve a variety of multiple intelligences (bodily/kinesthetic, spatial, linguistic, logical/mathematical).

Math Facts on the Floor!

One fun movement game involves use of a large piece of construction plastic (a shower curtain will do nicely). You should cut a piece of plastic in a square approximately six feet on a side. Across the top and down the side, write the numbers "0" through "9," thus forming a number grid. You may wish to station a student at each corner of the grid to keep it from moving. Next, you call out a math fact problem, and pairs of students (or individuals) have to move to the appropriate grid and call out the answer. For example, if a teacher calls out "5 × 6 = ?" the student will hop first on "5" then move down to the intersection with the 6s, while saying "5 × 6 = 30!" Having students work in pairs offers students the opportunity to discuss their answer before shouting it out. This is a great tear-out activity, and can be played by four students up to the entire class.

IDEAS FROM TEACHERS

Teaching Percentages

Students are often most motivated when they see that their educational activities can help them in real-world situations, such as shopping. In most shopping experiences, students confront percentages, and teachers can use shopping experiences as a teaching tool. To set up a lesson on percentages, teachers may bring in some old clothes on hangers and create a "Boutique." With only 12 to 20 items in the store, students can be challenged to learn percentages. First, place a price on each item and then place a percentage discount tag on each item. The discount tags could read "10% off," "25% off," and so forth. Each student will be responsible for recording a description of all pieces, the original price, and the final price after the discount.

Differentiated Tear Out Ideas for Percentages

For a tiered version of this activity, have students in one tear out group compute the final price, as described above, but add the percentage associated with the local tax on the item. Another idea would be to compute prices for a grocery list, complete with multiple items and percentage of tax for each.

TEACHING STRATEGY: THE ERRORLESS LEARNING PROCEDURES

The recent brain research—specifically the "emotional brain" basis of learning as discussed in Chapter 1—has emphasized that children require high levels of success in order to be motivated to continue their work in any curriculum area. There is no area of the curriculum in which this is truer than in math, because of the often negative emotional baggage associated with math in the elementary grades. Psychologists indicate that students need to succeed at least 85 percent of the time in order for learning to take place. With this emphasis on high levels of success, some theorists began to experiment with a number of techniques that resulted in high levels of success and few errors on the part of the students. The theorists postulated that learning would be less painful and more fun if it could be constructed to result in almost no errors. The resulting instructional procedures became known as errorless learning procedures (Wolery, Bailey, & Sugai, 1988).

> An errorless learning procedure is an instructional procedure that precludes students from performing an incorrect response. Thus the students experience much higher success in learning.

Like all behavioral instructional procedures, errorless learning is dependent upon accurate daily recording of the number of corrects and the number of errors a student achieves during the lesson. That record of success is necessary in order to assure that the student is learning the material in an errorless or nearly errorless fashion.

Wolery and colleagues (1988) presented a number of reasons for using errorless learning procedures. First, errorless learning is very efficient in that time is saved. This procedure usually results in mastery of material in considerably fewer instructional sessions than are required when other instructional procedures are used. Also, for general education classes, the errorless procedures may be used in a peer buddy fashion, making this a great tear out or mainline instructional activity for everyone in the class.

Next, these researchers suggest that errorless learning promotes positive social interaction between students. Using these procedures, very few errors are made, and much less social stigma is associated with any errors that do occur (Wolery et al., 1988). This makes the errorless learning procedure very effective as an interpersonal learning format in a differentiated math class. Also, errorless procedures should certainly be considered an option of choice for special education students working in inclusive classrooms. For these reasons, teachers should consider using errorless learning for many types of instruction in early math. Further, there are several errorless learning procedures available.

The Prompting Tactic

A prompt is defined as teacher or peer-tutor assistance before a student responds to a question. Prompts may be either verbal or gestural, and are used to increase the likelihood of correct response (Wolery et al., 1988). Further, if enough appropriate prompts are used to all but eliminate any common errors, and correct responses are sufficiently rewarded, prompting becomes an errorless learning technique. Thus, the student will master the math problems with very few errors.

An illustration may be helpful. If a student struggling in math has some difficulty with place value decisions (i.e., regrouping) in the addition of whole numbers, the teacher may present a series of double-digit addition problems written vertically like those below.

25	44	62	47
+37	+19	+34	+39

The child would have to discriminate between the problems that required regrouping and those that did not, as well as to solve the problems that required regrouping. In assisting the child to complete the problems, if the child summed the digits in the ones column and began to write a two-digit answer under that column rather than placing one digit at the top of the next column, the peer tutor or teacher may prompt the child by merely tapping the paper at the top of the next column to remind the student to write the number down in the tens place. This prompting procedure would tend to eliminate most errors (presuming that the child had previously acquired the prerequisite skills in math facts), and errorless learning would result. This type of tactic is very effective for differentiated classes that utilize a peer tutor or peer buddy instructional approach.

The Time Delay Tactic

Time delay is another errorless learning procedure; it was first introduced by Touchette (1971). The time delay procedure is implemented by presenting a series of problems to a student, verbally providing the answers to each problem, and increasing the amount of time between the problem and the answer (Schuster, Stevens, & Doak, 1990; Wolery, Cybriwsky, Gast, & Boyle-Gast, 1991). Schuster and colleagues (1990) provided an example of this procedure in teaching word recognition, but the same tactics have been applied to teach multiplication facts to students with learning disabilities (Koscinski & Gast, 1993). Further, time delay could easily be applied to teach virtually any other type of math problem across the elementary grades.

Schuster et al. (1990) used time delay to teach students with disabilities a set of vocabulary words and definitions. The teacher preselected 30 unknown words and their definitions from material the student would soon cover in the general education class, and presented these using the time delay tactic. The results showed drastic improvement in only a few days.

Implementation of Time Delay

Here is an example of how multiplication math facts may be taught using a time delay procedure coupled with peer buddy teaching in Mr. Varella's fourth-grade math class. Mr. Varella should preselect peer buddies based on common skills in multiplication math facts (or any other type of math problem). Students who need help with the five and six times tables should work together, while students who haven't mastered the eight and nine times tables should be partnered together. These peer buddies would work together for 20 minutes each day for a period of days on their math facts.

Mr. Varella would first need to teach the time delay procedure by modeling it for the class. He would select a student and work with that student doing a time delay instructional procedure with the class watching. Mr. Varella would present math facts to that student using flash cards that showed the math fact on the front (e.g., $4 \times 8 = \underline{\hspace{1cm}}$), and the math fact with the answer on the back ($4 \times 8 = 32$). During the first instructional session, a 0-second time delay is used—this means there would be zero seconds between when Mr. Varella presents the problem and when he verbally reads the problem and the answer. Specifically, Mr. Varella would hold up a flashcard with the math fact on it (so that the student could view the side without the answer), and immediately Mr. Varella would read the equation and the answer; thus there are zero seconds between the math fact being presented visually to the student and the student's receiving the verbal prompt. Mr. Varella shows the card and says, "4×8 is 32." The student would then repeat, "4×8 is 32." Mr. Varella would then show the reverse side of the card to the student, as feedback on the student's correctness. Mr. Varella would also place a slash mark by the "$4 \times 8 = $" equation under the "correct wait" column on the daily score sheet such as the one presented on the next page. This mark indicates that the student waited to hear the answer and then correctly restated the problem and answer. Mr. Varella would present all ten facts twice using the zero-second time delay in order to assist the student in learning the facts. Thus, there will be 20 marks on the score sheet by that point.

Time Delay Score Sheet for Eight Times Tables

Student's Name _____   Date _____   Time Delay _____

Math Fact	Corrects		Errors		
	Anticipations	Waits	Anticipations	Waits	Nonresponse
$8 \times 1 = 8$					
$8 \times 2 = 16$					
$8 \times 3 = 24$					
$8 \times 4 = 32$					
$8 \times 5 = 40$					
$8 \times 6 = 48$					
$8 \times 7 = 56$					
$8 \times 8 = 64$					
$8 \times 9 = 72$					
$8 \times 10 = 80$					

When that was completed, Mr. Varella would present the facts with a three-second delay between presentation of the flash card and the correct completion of the equation.

The student should be encouraged to read the equation and give the answer before the teacher does if he or she knows the answer. Otherwise, the student should be instructed to wait until the verbal prompt. Mr. Varella would then mark that as a "correct anticipation." If the student does not know the answer, but waits for the teacher's verbal prompt and then repeats the equation correctly, the student should be rewarded with a mark in the "correct wait" column. Each "correct anticipation" would be noted with a check mark by Mr. Varella. Each correct wait would be noted with a slash mark. Other responses would be noted with an "x." Mr. Varella would again present all of the facts in the four's times tables twice, using the three-second delay, and thus 40 slash marks would be present on the child's score sheet at the end of the instructional session. The student's "correct waits" and "correct anticipations" should be charted daily, since increasing the "correct anticipations" is the overall goal of the procedure. Also, charting both correct waits and correct anticipations emphasizes for the student that both of these are correct—hence the term *errorless learning*.

On the next day, Mr. Varella should consider using a zero-second delay for only one presentation of the ten math facts in the eight's times tables, and thus to use a three-second delay for the presentation of those math facts three times. The student's progress, or lack thereof, will assist in making that determination. Finally, on the third day, pending appropriate student progress, only the three-second time delay is used. The ten facts are, again, presented four times each, and the student's score is again tallied and charted.

The chart opposite presents a relatively standard recording format. Note that each type of student response is listed in the five columns so that the teacher can note the specific type of response made. "Waits" indicate that the child waited to hear the prompt from the teacher before responding; "anticipations" indicate that the child did not wait for the verbal prompt from the teacher. For both the anticipations and the waits, the child could possibly answer either correctly or incorrectly. Alternatively, the child might not verbally respond at all. Thus, there are five possible answers: the terms used for these five possibilities are *correct anticipations, correct waits, anticipation error, wait error,* and *nonresponse.* Obviously, the goal of the teacher is to increase correct anticipations and decrease all other responses until the child performs with 100 percent accuracy and all of the corrects are anticipations rather than waits. Note that the child "feels" rewarded for correct waits also, thus assuring an experience of success for the student. The emotional impact of such errorless learning in math cannot be overstated.

Time delay works particularly well in the differentiated math class when the teacher couples this tactic with a peer tutoring strategy, such as the class-wide peer tutoring strategy described later in this chapter. Once Mr. Varella has demonstrated this with himself as the tutor, he should also demonstrate how the roles of tutor and tutee may be reversed. In other words, the student who was formerly the tutee now presents the math facts flash cards to Mr. Varella, and the student is taught to mark a daily score sheet for Mr. Varella's success. From that point on, it is fairly easy, even in the lower grade levels, to teach students to tutor each other. Ideally, once the students in the class learn this procedure, they can serve equally well as tutors or tutees, and they will typically serve in each role each day. Students should be tutored on math facts for approximately ten minutes and then should serve as tutees for their peer buddies for an additional ten minutes. Using this tactic in the differentiated class will not only strengthen interpersonal intelligence, it will also involve all students in meaningful tutoring roles and will make mathematics much less emotionally threatening for many struggling learners.

Uses of Time Delay Across Grade Levels

Research results indicate that students in elementary general education classes quickly mastered almost any material presented to them using this errorless learning procedure (Schuster et al., 1990; Wolery et al., 1991). Also, maintenance probes indicated that the students' mastery of factual material has been maintained for more than three months as a result of time delay instruction. Again, for almost any type of elementary math problem, consistent use of the time delay procedure would result in building automaticity and consistently high performance in a nonthreatening way.

Furthermore, time delay may be used in higher grade levels as well. For example, recent research has indicated that factual material from various curriculum areas in higher grades can be mastered by the use of time delay. For example, Wolery and his coworkers (1991) used time delay to assist adolescents with learning disabilities to master factual material from their content secondary curriculum areas. In that particular study, the content included the functions of federal offices, the services provided by local offices and agencies, over-the-counter medications, and the effects of specific vitamins and minerals on the body. As these diverse topics indicate, any curricula that can be specified as isolated factual material can be structured as curricula for a time delay procedure, including higher grade mathematics content.

A Cover, Copy, Compare Tactic

A final errorless learning procedure that results in high success in math is the cover, copy, compare tactic. Stading, Williams, and McLaughlin (1996) used this errorless learning technique to teach multiplication math facts to a third-grade student with a learning disability. In this procedure, the student is presented with a set of math fact equations to be mastered—perhaps the seven's multiplication and division facts. These equations should be written on flash cards that contain a math fact equation and the answer. The student then performs each task: Copy, cover, compare.

When presented with one of the flash cards, the student first copies the equation and the answer while reading it aloud. Next, the student covers the problem by turning the flash card facedown and covering his or her written equation with a cover sheet, and then writes the equation from memory. Finally, the student compares the two written equations. This is a fairly simple errorless learning procedure that students can accomplish by themselves. Also, working with the flash cards makes this a bit more "manipulative" than merely presenting the same math facts on a worksheet.

SUMMARY: ERRORLESS LEARNING

As these several errorless learning procedures demonstrate, students can master the basic math facts, as well as even more complicated math problems, in a errorless or near errorless fashion. In fact, this procedure repeatedly has been shown to be successful in both special and general education math classes (Stading et al., 1996; Wolery et al., 1988).

> Errorless learning, unlike almost all other instructional ideas, can help to alleviate the fear of math that is demonstrated by many students. Thus, this procedure can increase students' enjoyment of mathematics.

However, there is one critically important additional advantage to using errorless learning procedures in math.

As described previously, the emerging brain research has demonstrated convincingly that when students fear a particular subject, they are much less likely to be actively engaged in that subject or to master the content (Sousa, 2001). Given the fear many students experience in math class, teachers of mathematics have a unique responsibility to address this emotional baggage, and errorless learning can be a critically important instructional approach in the differentiated classroom for that reason. One may wistfully only imagine the public school math classes that could be possible if every single student was initially taught in an errorless learning—and thus a much less threatening—fashion. Perhaps students would then experience the joy and beauty of mathematical problem solving, as math teachers wish they would experience it.

TEACHING STRATEGY: CLASSWIDE PEER TUTORING FOR DIFFERENTIATED INSTRUCTION

You may not have realized it, but in the discussion of errorless learning above each reader received a highly practical instructional strategy idea that will make differentiated learning activities not only possible in the average-sized general education class, but also quite fun. Embedded within the discussion of errorless learning (see the description of time delay) was an applied description of an instructional approach for differentiating the general education classroom that is referred to as classwide peer tutoring. In this system all students in the class learn to tutor each other, and this provides a wonderful opportunity for both mainline instruction and tear out group work (Allsopp, 1997; Greenwood, Delquadri, & Hall, 1989).

For the past two decades a number of researchers, principally led by Dr. Charles Greenwood at the University of Kansas in Kansas City, have developed a system of peer buddy tutoring that can easily be employed in elementary classes of almost any size (Allsopp, 1997; Greenwood et al., 1989; Mortweet et al., 1999). This procedure served as the basis for the discussion of the time delay strategy above, in which students who are paired together serve the role of both tutor and tutee in the class.

Although classwide peer tutoring should not be used for initial instruction in any type of math problem, this type of instruction is very useful during the guided practice and independent practice phases of instruction in math. In fact, this instructional model may be more helpful than traditional instruction for monitoring student progress since a record is kept of all errors each student makes. The teacher can review this record outside of daily class time and make determinations about an individual student's level of understanding of the math problems. Should a student be struggling, that will quickly become apparent in his or her daily worksheet scores.

> Knowing how to employ a classwide peer tutoring program can, in a very real sense, make a highly differentiated math class possible, since the teacher will then be serving as a facilitator of the math lesson rather than as the instructional leader for the entire class.

Essentially, in classwide peer tutoring, some time—perhaps 20 minutes—is set aside each day for the tutoring experience. The students are paired together (teachers should vary these pairs daily) and provided with the appropriate materials for the tutoring session—typically either flashcards or a worksheet that involves only one specific type of problem (e.g., two-digit addition with regrouping). During a tutoring session, one student will first serve as the "tutor" and will record the corrects and errors of the "tutee." The tutor will present math facts, equations, or problems on flash cards to the other student and record the responses. When the problems are presented on a worksheet, the tutor is still responsible for marking the daily record of errors. When a worksheet is used, each student should be provided a copy—the tutee completes the problems while the tutor marks correct or incorrect on his or her worksheet.

The tutee is awarded two points for correct answers. Should an error be made, the tutor can assist the student in figuring out the problem, and upon correction of the problem the tutee is awarded one point. Zero points are awarded for non-responses. Should the tutor and tutee both need assistance, they are instructed to raise their hands to request help. After ten minutes, the roles will be switched for each pair of students (i.e., the tutor becomes the tutee), and the new tutor begins to record the progress of the tutee. Of course, each student's progress is charted each day, and students are typically highly motivated to improve their scores over previous performance. During the 20-minute tutoring time, the teacher should move throughout the class and assist students as necessary. The teacher thus becomes a facilitator of learning, which frees the teacher for more in-depth, one-on-one instruction for students who need extra help. Moreover, teachers are responsible for setting up the classwide peer tutoring setting. This is accomplished by consideration of only three things:

1. Close examination and/or specific assessment that will depict the exact skill level of every child in the class so that specific types of math problems may be identified and either flashcards or worksheets can be developed for those problems. These flashcards or worksheets should include only those specific types of problems on which the student has received initial instruction but has not mastered.

> Perhaps more than any other strategy in this text, the classwide peer tutoring strategy should be mastered and used by every general education teacher in the elementary and middle grades. This tactic, in a very concrete sense, makes differentiated instruction possible, because it allows teachers to truly individualize their lessons for classes of 20 or even 30 kids.

2. The development of daily recording sheets that allow the tutor to record the correct and error responses on the specific math problems for the student he or she is tutoring. For worksheet-based activities, the teacher can review the copy of each student's worksheet after class and analyze any errors that were made.

3. A training period in which the teacher demonstrates how the tutoring should be done. This should emphasize the reciprocal nature of the tutoring—that is, that each student serves as both tutor and tutee each and every day.

At this point, you may wish to reread the discussion of the time delay tactic. In that section, you can see the relatively easy application of this research-proven instructional method for the differentiated class.

Most of the research on classwide peer tutoring has been undertaken in elementary general education classes and concentrated on reading and language arts subject areas. Nevertheless, this teaching procedure has been shown to be effective in math (Allsopp, 2003; Mortweet et al., 1999), and application of this tactic for almost any type of math problem during the elementary grades would be quite easy. The tactic is also useful in the upper grade levels, as far as secondary school (Allsopp, 1999), so upper elementary and middle school teachers should learn and begin to employ this highly practical strategy.

WHAT'S NEXT?

As young math scholars move from the early grades into Grades 4 through 6, the demands of the mathematics curriculum change from mastery of the mechanics of mathematical operations to increasingly applied use of math. The next chapter will focus on tactics teachers may use as students explore mathematical applications.

Differentiating for Conceptual Development and Deep Understanding

CONSTRUCTIVIST THEORY AND UNDERSTANDING OF MATHEMATICS

Embedded within the National Council of Teachers of Mathematics (NCTM; 2000) standards is a strong emphasis on developing an in-depth understanding of mathematics, and many practitioners have suggested that constructivist theory might be the most appropriate perspective from which to develop deep conceptual understanding in math across the grade levels (Grobecker, 1999; Jones, Wilson, & Bhojwani, 1997; Woodward & Montague, 2002). Constructivist theory calls for students to be perceived as learners who may be immature in their mathematical understandings, but who can develop in-depth understandings as long as they:

1. Have mastered the prerequisite skills for a particular problem and

2. Are supported by the teacher and curriculum as they "construct" further understandings of the mathematics problems under study.

In the constructivist view, teachers are facilitators who provide appropriate supports to assist students in developing their growing understandings of various mathematical skills. Further, as students mature in their cognitive understandings of mathematics concepts, the teacher should withdraw the supports and allow students to work more independently.

According to this perspective, in order to accomplish effective instruction teachers need to develop an array of instructional skills. First, teachers must understand what supports a student may need based on the student's current understanding of the problem. Next, the teacher must apply that type and level of support, and at a later point withdraw it as student comprehension increases. Closely aligned with this perspective is the notion of guiding the cognitive understandings of students as they develop in their mathematical experiences (Alsup, 2003).

> The constructivist approach suggests that teachers cannot transmit mathematic knowledge directly to students; rather teachers can lead or guide students in their mathematical understanding and thus equip students to discover the mathematical principles and concepts for themselves.

Teachers do this "guiding" by listening to a student's solution to a problem and then asking pointed topical questions that are designed to guide students cognitively through the problem solution process. Thus, students are responsible for using the information they have learned to solve the problem, and students are exposed to the mystery and the fun of problem solution in math. Students may use manipulatives or models as described in previous chapters in order to solve the problem, but the emphasis will be on moving students past the necessity for concrete or semi-concrete models and into a deeper level of understanding. The next section offers several examples of the use of movements, chants, and the like, which can cognitively guide students' understandings of various mathematical concepts in the elementary grades. These ideas are compatible with both constructivist theory and brain-compatible research.

IDEAS FROM TEACHERS

The "Geometry With Ribbons" Tactic

When working with geometric shapes, teachers can easily guide students' concept mastery by using a movement and hands-on activity. Teachers should stand students in the positions of the shapes to be studied. For example, a square, a rectangle, and a parabola can be demonstrated by four students with ribbons. First, cut four ribbons approximately six feet in length, and tie a knot in the middle of each ribbon. To begin the activity, tell two students to face each other about three feet apart and to hold one end of two different ribbons with their right hands. One of those two students should hold the end of another ribbon with his or her left hand. To form the square, two other students should take hold of the ribbons in the right hands of the first two students, and walk away from the students (teachers should coach them to depart at a 90° angle), allowing their ribbon to flow through their hands until they reach the knot. Next, under the teacher's coaching, the student from the first pair who is holding only one ribbon takes hold of the ribbon held by the other student in the first pair and walks away while flowing the ribbon through his or her hand until reaching the knot. To finish making the square, the teacher then offers a final ribbon to the second pair of students. Thus, the ribbons have formed a square that is three feet long on each side.

At this point, the teacher should point out the features of the square (all sides the same length, 90° angles, etc.). To turn this into a rectangle, merely have two adjacent students holding knots walk away from the square flowing the ribbon until they reach the end. To form the parabola, merely have two adjacent students change to acute angles.

IDEAS FROM TEACHERS

Teaching About Circles

This is both a movement-based and a rhythm-based tactic to teach terms associated with a circle (*circumference, radius,* and *diameter*). Both movement and rhythmic chanting are used. First, emphasize that the lesson will teach the students about circles. Next, teach the chant, and finally have the students master the movements described below. The chant uses the rhythm "We will, we will rock you!" In the timing of saying "We will, we will rock you!" one time through, use the following chant.

> This is circumference, all around the side.
> Next comes radius, middle to the side.
> Next is diameter, all the way through!
> All of that's a circle, I'll show it to you.

Have 16 or so students do the chant above while remaining still and standing in a line. When they begin the chant the second time, have them move to demonstrate the specific terms used. First, when chanting about the circle, have students move forward, with the first nine students forming a circle by holding hands. When the chant begins to discuss radius, have another line of two students move into the circle under the upraised hands of those forming the circumference and, while holding hands only with each other, move into the center. The first student should stop at the center point. Finally, the last five students should enter the circle from a different direction and move across the circle to demonstrate diameter.

A Differentiated Tear Out Idea for the Circle Activity

One way to vary the complexity of this activity is to use strings with knots in them to demonstrate where students should be for some groups of students. This has the overall effect of "tiering" this activity and making it a bit simpler. Cut three pieces of string or ribbon to the expected lengths of the circumference, the radius, and the diameter. Along each piece of string, at approximately the position at which each student will eventually stand, teachers may tie a knot to remind students that there should be nine students in the circumference, two in the radius, five in the diameter, and so on.

A Cognitive Guided Visualization Strategy

Perhaps an example of cognitive guided inquiry would assist. Visualization is one method by which students can learn to problem solve in mathematics. Further, a visualization tactic that is creatively guided by the teacher can help students bridge the gap between concrete or semi-concrete thinking and more abstract problem solving. In fact, teaching children how to visualize math problems when problem solving can help them to make sense of the problem and develop increased abstract thinking ability. Visualization is a tactic that is being used increasingly in math because—as pointed out in Chapter 1—mathematical understandings are often related to increased activity in the visual areas of the brain (Sousa, 2001). Thus, the intentional construction of an "image" of the problem will typically enhance a student's understanding of the problem.

Behrend (2003) recently suggested a cognitive guided inquiry method to assist students in visualizing problems. All children, including children who may struggle in math, have some natural problem-solving abilities, and Behrend suggests that teachers begin with the problem-solving strategies that students generate naturally. From that basis, teachers will use a series of focused questions to help students visualize the problem more completely. In this technique, the teacher asks focused questions that draw the students' attention to various aspects of the math problem. As an example, a series of such focused questions is presented in the teacher–student dialogue below.

A Cognitive Guided Visualization Dialogue

Problem:

"Maria has 4 bags of cookies. There are 3 cookies in each bag. How many cookies in all?"

Dialogue:

Teacher: "Jay, tell me about how you got your answer of seven."

Jay: "I didn't really know how to do it so I said four and three makes seven so seven is my answer."

Teacher: "Does that tell you how many cookies there are? Would you like me to read the problem again?"

Jay: "OK."

Teacher: "Think about it. There are four bags of cookies. Got that in your head?"

Jay: "Yeah." (He might grab for counters)

Teacher: "And there are three cookies in each bag."

Jay: "Three in each bag?"

Teacher: "Yes, three cookies in each bag."

Jay: "OK, so I need some more of these [counters]."

(Jay puts three "cookies" in each of four "bags" represented by circles on a piece of paper.)

Teacher: "So, how many cookies are there?"

(Jay counts the "cookies" and finds that . . .)

Jay: "There are twelve cookies!"

Teacher: "That's right! There are twelve cookies in all."

USING COGNITIVE GUIDED VISUALIZATION

As shown in this dialogue, the visualization begins with students' natural attempts to problem solve. Next, teachers should ask focused questions to assist students in understanding the problem more thoroughly in order to help them visualize it. Over time, being reminded of the conditions in a particular type of problem coupled with visualization of the problem will strengthen a student's problem-solving ability. The use of visualization also helps students generalize these newly awakened problem-solving strategies. Further, focusing on problem visualization even allows students to solve multiple-step problems that include extraneous information, because the visualization assists students to attend to only relevant information (Behrend, 2003; Carpenter, Fennema, & Franke, 1996).

> When using cognitively guided visualization, group work is more effective than individual instruction, since students are encouraged to share their responses and their visualizations with other students.

Hopefully, instead of automatically assuming that their own answer is wrong—as do many struggling students—students will become more confident in justifying how they arrived at their own answer. When students explain their own answers to others, they and others can often spot errors that have been made and correct them. The group work basis of this tactic makes it very effective in a differentiated math class, as either a tear out tactic or as a tactic for use with the mainline instructional group.

Implementation of Cognitive Guided Visualization

The implementation of cognitively guided visualization is simple, but will be different for every student or group of students. First, working in a small tear out group, the teacher would provide a problem for the students to consider.

Next, the teacher should allow students to solve the problem in their own way. Then, the teacher will have the students share the strategies they used. Finally, using focused questions with students who got an incorrect answer, the teacher should guide them through the visualization process to arrive at the correct answer. In fact, after students have participated in this method, it should be possible for the teacher to use students for the final step above—having students ask the "guiding" questions. Initially, this should be done under the supervision of the teacher, but as students become fluent in this technique, it is possible to use this in a tear out group, with an experienced student doing the guiding.

Behrend (2003) used this strategy to assess whether visualization would foster more accurate problem solving in two elementary age students who were having difficulty in math. The two students explored a problem similar to the one in the dialogue above, and each devised a strategy to answer the problem. Each answer was incorrect. By encouraging one student's desire to explore mathematics and teaching the other student to "think more and guess less," Behrend demonstrated that those students with math deficits could be taught to use visualization to make sense of the word problems. They learned how to model the problem situation using manipulatives to aid their own visualization, and were thus more actively engaged in the problem than they would have been had the problem been presented merely as a paper-and-pencil task. Further, when errors were made, they were able to realize where and why their own problem solving broke down and to see how to solve future problems correctly.

Cognitive guided inquiry and visualization are techniques that can assist students in moving from concrete or representational mathematics toward more abstract thinking. Also, research has shown that these techniques result in greater conceptual understanding of math than merely rote memory or static, "practice sheet" types of instruction. Clearly, this is the direction recommended within the recently published mathematics standards (Grobecker, 1999; NCTM, 2000). For these reasons, teachers moving into differentiated instruction should explore the use of this cognitively guided visualization tactic.

SCAFFOLDED INSTRUCTION IN MATH

Scaffolded instruction is a newly developed instructional technique used in many different subjects, including math (Woodward & Montague, 2002). Scaffolded instruction was developed within the constructivist perspective described previously, and represents a way for teachers to strategically question students in order to assist students in building their understanding of a math problem. Scaffolded instruction, then, may best be understood as a sequence of prompted content, materials, and teacher or peer support to facilitate learning (Grobecker, 1999; Karp & Voltz, 2000; Larkin, 2001). In fact, the cognitively guided visualization tactic described above is an excellent example of a scaffolded instruction technique.

Implementation of Scaffolded Instruction

In scaffolded instruction, the emphasis is placed on a teacher's assisting the student in the learning process with individual prompting and guidance that is tailored to the specific needs of the individual student and offers just enough support (i.e., a scaffold) for the student in a new task (Karp & Voltz, 2000). The student is initially considered an apprentice in the learning effort.

Clearly, the level of support must be specifically tailored to the student's ever-changing understanding of the math problem. Further, that support should gradually be withdrawn, allowing the student to eventually "own" the task performance. Larkin (2001) presented several guidelines for implementing scaffolded instruction.

> Less-than-adequate support in learning a math concept leaves the student stranded and unable to comprehend the assigned work and complete the task. Too much support, on the other hand, would prevent the student from independently mastering the math concept.

TEACHING TACTICS

GUIDELINES FOR EFFECTIVE SCAFFOLDING

Identify what students know. Effective scaffolding requires that teachers are cognizant of what a student already knows (background or prior knowledge) and of the student's misconceptions (i.e., which competencies are developing and which are beyond the student's current level of functioning). For example, one teacher was aware that some of her students "think in terms of money." Therefore, when she taught "rounding" to those students, she used the familiar concept of money.

Begin with what students can do. One special education teacher was aware of individual student ability levels. When she began reading word problems, she gave the students with difficulties in math an opportunity to read a simple problem independently or with a little teacher assistance. This enabled students to begin the word problem lesson successfully.

Help students achieve success quickly. Another teacher found that writing and penmanship tasks in math were laborious for some of her students with written expression disabilities. When she first taught math problems, she assisted her students in the general education classroom by having students dictate their ideas while she or a peer buddy wrote them on paper. This accommodation enabled the students who had difficulty with written expression to generate ideas on solving the problems without worrying about how to convey them on paper.

Help students to "be" like everyone else. Many students who struggle with math express a desire to be regarded like other students. Therefore, teachers should orient classroom tasks such that each student's work is perceived as similar to the work of his or her peers. For example, one teacher in an inclusive math class suggested that a struggling student be moved into a grade level text like that of his peers. The teacher informed the student of his

(Continued)

(Continued)

responsibility to work hard, but also let him know that she would be there to give him the assistance he needed. When placed in a grade-appropriate text and relying heavily on teacher assistance, he was still struggling with math but holding his own. Further, the student felt good about using the same book as his fifth-grade peers.

Know when it's time to stop. Many teachers have learned from experience that continued drill and practice might not always be effective. Once students demonstrate mastery of a skill, continued practice may result in their refusing to work or producing work with numerous errors. Tear out activities are essential for these students, since they keep students focused on the same type of task in math, but typically at a more challenging level. Scaling back on the practice problems can also help. For example, in one class when students were asked to complete a general education math assignment with 50 problems, the teacher noted that some students completed the first three rows of problems without an error, but began to make errors in later rows of problems. This teacher reduced the number of assigned practice problems, and noted that this effectively reduced the errors for those students.

Help students be independent when they have command of the activity. Effective scaffolding means that teachers need to listen and watch for clues from their students as to when teacher assistance is or is not needed. Obviously, teachers do not want students to fail, but they should not allow students to become too dependent on the teacher. Further, achieving independence is different for individual students. Some students may be at identical skill levels, but emotionally they may be at different levels regarding the amount of frustration they can tolerate in their math class. Therefore, all students may not be ready to be weaned from teacher assistance at the same time. In other words, some students will need more teacher support while learning to perform a task; others will demonstrate task mastery more quickly. Like the mother bird that helps her chicks leave the nest to become independent birds, teachers need to help their students gradually move from teacher assistance to student independence as students demonstrate command of the math task.

SOURCE: Adapted from Larkin, 2001.

IDEAS FROM TEACHERS

Teaching About Fractions

Musical Notes as "Scaffolded Fractions"

Teaching fractions can be challenging, and use of scaffolds can greatly assist some students. One idea for teaching fractions initially is the presentation of a "tree" of musical notes. The teacher can make a "fraction tree" that will ultimately be shaped something like a Christmas tree. A single whole note should be presented at the top of the tree, with two half notes below it. The teacher can explain that the half notes are not as long as the whole note, and the students can see the difference. Teachers who can sing may wish to "sing" a whole note to show the difference vocally between it and the two half notes. Thus, the students will both see and hear the differences between these notes. The teacher can then lead a dialogue on those distinctions.

The tree also represents the fact that two half notes make a whole note, just like two halves make a whole, and the teacher should point that out. Next, below the half notes the teacher should present quarter notes, eighth notes, and even sixteenth notes. Of course, this doesn't teach all fractions, but it does illustrate the general concepts of parts making a whole. Images such as this provide wonderful scaffolds for students who need additional help with fractions.

Eat the Teaching Tool! Fractions Using Pizzas!

Many teachers use manipulatives to teach fractions (sections of pie, etc.). One memorable variation on that idea is to use sections of a pizza! While this costs a bit (unless you can get help from the school cafeteria), it provides a memorable lesson on fractions.

DEBATE ON WHAT A SCAFFOLD IS

There has been considerable discussion in the literature concerning what scaffolding is and is not (Woodward & Montague, 2002). Some view scaffolded instruction exclusively as interaction with a teacher who can provide individually tailored support for individual student learning (Karp & Voltz, 2000). These theorists see the critical component of scaffolding as the sensitivity of the adult who is supporting the student in the learning process.

Others, however, take a broader view and consider scaffolding to be any specific learning support, whether from another individual or not; thus scaffolded instruction in this view may come from a cue card identifying steps toward problem solution rather than individual help from another person (Woodward & Montague, 2002). From this perspective, various charts and/or graphics that assist in the learning process would be considered scaffolds that the student—using adult supervision initially—could use to master newly presented subject matter. Regardless of how this debate turns out, all theorists are in general agreement that the provision of supports for students' learning of new concepts is critical. Several tactics are presented below that may serve as scaffolds for many students who are struggling in math.

A Word Problem Map Tactic

One example of such a scaffold is the *Word Problem Map*. As noted throughout this text, many students with learning difficulties in math have problems organizing their thoughts during any learning task; this can be devastating to students' efforts to comprehend math word problems. These students may not understand that in most word problems there is an underlying structure that can be identified, and that identification of this structure can assist in problem solution. A number of researchers have encouraged specific instruction in identification of the overall structure of the math problem for students who are struggling in math (Gagnon & Maccini, 2001).

Teaching Cue Words

In developing a map of a word problem, identification of the cue words is the first step. In almost all word problems certain terms are used that are suggestive of various operations, and word problems generally involve translation of these cue words into mathematical operations. Many teachers find that students are more motivated when they are taught that solving word problems really involves a "secret code" or set of cue words that the teacher can teach them. Although these words do not always have the same meaning in all word problems, the teacher can assure students that the words often indicate a particular operation. The list of cue words below may be helpful, although it is not an exhaustive list.

TEACHING TACTICS

CUE WORDS IN WORD PROBLEMS

Operation	Terms Used	Example
Addition	altogether, add, how many, put together, in all	When they put together the marbles, how many were there?
Subtraction	take, took away, left, gave away	How many did they take home?
Multiplication	Problems that tell about one and then ask for total	Each tree limb weighed 40 pounds. How much did four limbs weigh?
Division	Problems that tell about many and then ask about one	Five bags of candy cost 25 cents. How much was each bag?

Initially, during instruction involving cue words, the teacher should select only problems in which the cue words mean the operation specified above. The student should be trained to write a "number sentence" to represent a single operation problem. Then multiple operation problems that require multiple number sentences are introduced. When grading this work, teachers may wish to assign a certain number of points to correctly identifying this number sentence independent of points awarded for problem solution.

Teachers using the cue word strategy for word problems should prepare a poster of these cue words and place it in front of the class, and refer to it often when discussing word problems. When a word problem is initially read in class, the teacher should challenge the students to find the cue words in the problem. Each of those should then be investigated to determine its meaning in that particular problem.

Finally, teachers should require that students complete some problems in which the cue words represent different operations from those they typically represent, and offer instruction on how the meaning was changed based on sentence construction in the problem. Initially, the teacher should present a simple word problem. Here is an example:

Both Alonzo and his sister, Mia, had an opportunity from the teacher at school to take home some extra crackers. Now, Alonzo knew that his Mom loved him and worked hard to feed the family each day, so he decided he'd bring her 10 crackers to show his love in return. From his teacher, he took 14 crackers, and Mia picked up 6 more. When Alonzo told Mia about his plans to give some crackers to Mom, he and Mia agreed to add their crackers together, take 10 crackers home for their Mom, and split the rest. With that in mind, how many crackers could each one eat before getting home?

Next, the teacher should ask the students what words in the problem might be cues to how to solve the problem. The students and teacher should note the terms (more, how many, add). The teacher may wish to discuss that the term *more* may often mean addition, as it does here, whereas phrases like "how many could each one eat" might suggest subtraction.

Differentiated Tear Out Activities for Cue Words in Word Problems

After that introduction and before the teacher led instruction, the teacher should use the Guess, Assess, and Tear Out Tactic described previously to identify a group of students for a differentiated activity. While the teacher conducts the lesson for the remaining students in the mainline group, the tear out group could do a related activity. These activities may include the following:

1. A subgroup "analyzes" a different problem by noting the cue words in the problem. Depending on the level of the group overall, the teacher may provide a tiered version of this activity by either providing the list of cue words to the students in this group or not doing so. Later in the lesson, that problem could be used as a class illustration.

2. Another tear out group may be instructed to make up two new word problems, using a minimum of two of the cue words in each problem from the list of cue words presented above. Next, that group should solve the problems before presenting them to the class.

Moving From Cue Words to the Word Problem Map

The search for cue words and the other typical problem components may be formulated into a *Word Problem Map* similar to a story map used in reading instruction (Gagnon & Maccini, 2001). Whereas a story map in reading may be used to highlight the story structure (introduction, plot line or problem, characters, story climax, etc.), the word problem map is intended to assist the student with a learning problem in math to organize his or her thoughts concerning the structure of the word problem. Thus, when a student with problems in math reads a math problem in the general education classroom, he or she should simultaneously complete the word problem map as a scaffold on which to build understanding of that story.

While study of the structure of math problems can take place in a variety of ways, some methods are more complicated than others. The word problem map presented below is one of the simpler methods for providing students with a "scaffold" to assist in their understanding of simple word problems.

TEACHING TACTICS

A WORD PROBLEM MAP

Name: _____   Date: _____   Problem Number: _____

What type of problem is this?

_____

_____

The problem asked for what information?

_____

_____

What cue words were used?

_____

_____

These cue words suggest what operations?

_____

_____

Is there a particular order in which I must perform these operations?

_____

_____

(At this point the student should attempt the problem)

Did I get an answer that seems correct?

_____

_____

Have I re-checked the problem to make certain I understand it, and is there anything I missed?

_____

This word problem map activity is also very effective when completed as a buddy activity; two or three students may partner together to complete the map. Furthermore, these word problem maps should be reviewed in class as a post-problem activity to check for accuracy and for comprehension of the problem. Next, the word problem map may be adapted as necessary across the grade levels, and teachers should feel free to implement this in any fashion they desire that works for their students. Finally, the word problem map can be used as a study guide for any future tests on that content. In fact, a wide variety of instructional activities can be built around the word problem map concept.

GRAPHIC REPRESENTATIONS OF WORD PROBLEM SCHEMAS

Another form of scaffold is the use of graphic representations to represent math problems (Allsopp, 1999; Jitendra, 2002). In many ways, this is similar to both the visualization technique and the word problem map technique described above. Students using the graphic representation idea, however, are encouraged to draw their visualization of the math problem in a "hard copy" form, rather than use a prepared form or set of questions. This technique can greatly assist students with a strength in visual-spatial thinking.

In the graphic representation tactic, students are encouraged to identify and use the separate features of each problem, such as problems involving changing sums, grouping sets of objects together, or comparison of different sets. These problem types are referred to as different "schemas." A schema may be defined as a mental diagram or concept for a particular aspect of the problem (Jitendra, 2002). Next, students use schematic diagrams to represent the different aspects of the problem (Jitendra, 2002). Here are several examples.

TEACHING TACTICS

SAMPLE SCHEMATIC DIAGRAMS FOR WORD PROBLEMS

The Change Schema

One type of problem requires a change schema. These problems include a set of information that indicates change in other information in the problem.

John had some apples. Paul gave him 13 more apples. Now John has 17 apples. How many did John have in the beginning?

The change information (13 apples) must be subtracted from the total resultant set of information (17) in order to determine the start set. This change problem may be represented as follows.

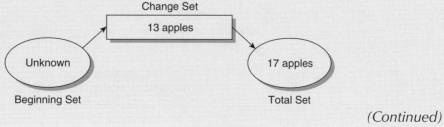

(Continued)

(Continued)

The Group Schema

In a group schema, items are grouped together from various sets. Consider the following problem:

Tiffany owns 13 blouses that she wears to school. Her twin sister Tammy owns 13 blouses. When these girls swap cloths for school, how many blouses can they choose from?

A group schema would be represented as follows.

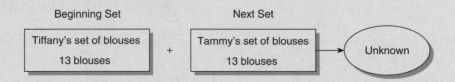

The Comparison Schema

Some word problems present "comparison" problems, which require the student to determine and subsequently compare values.

John has 6 computer games. He has 3 more than Paul. How many games does Paul have?

In order to solve this problem, the child must have a comparison schema or mental concept that includes three pieces of information: two reference quantities (the number of computer games that John has, and the difference) and a derived piece of information involving the comparison answer. Note also that the cue word *more* usually means that a child should add, but in this example it indicates subtraction.

A comparison schema would be represented as follows:

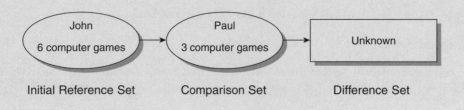

USING A REPRESENTATIONAL STRATEGY

As with many strategies presented in this text, there are different cognitive levels of the graphic representation strategy, making it appropriate for different grade levels. For younger students or students who may be less mature in their mathematical understandings, teachers will merely tell students what type of problem each is, and then present a pre-drawn graphic representation for that type of problem. The students would then write the appropriate information from the problem on the graphic representation. Using the designs above can greatly assist struggling students in their comprehension of math problems. For older, mathematically mature students, teachers should spend more time actually teaching students to recognize the different types of problem schemas. This in-depth instruction on the type of word problem is called *schema-based instruction* (Jitendra, 2002) and is discussed more fully in the next chapter.

The use of a graphic representation strategy has a number of advantages. Using graphic representations, like many of the strategies discussed in Chapter 3, assists the students in forming a picture of the math problem. According to the brain-compatible learning perspective described in Chapter 1, this tactic will empower students to actively engage the visualization areas within their brain. Also, unlike the visualization tactic described above, students doing graphic representation are actually drawing or filling in a graphic picture of the problem, which provides a hard copy for later use as a study guide.

Implementation of Graphic Representation

Using the graphic representation tactic is fairly straightforward once students are acquainted with the concept. Jitendra (2002) presented the following guidelines for student use in developing the representation itself. In application of the graphic representation tactic, teachers should plan on using this specific tactic over a period of several weeks in order for students to internalize these deeper understandings.

TEACHING TACTICS

GUIDELINES FOR DEVELOPING A GRAPHIC REPRESENTATION OF A WORD PROBLEM

Problem Schema Identification and Representation

1. Find the problem pattern

   a. Read the problem carefully
   b. Ask whether the problem requires changing, grouping, or comparing (think about the overall schema of the problem)

2. Organize the problem within a diagram

   a. Map the known information on the diagram (write it in!)
   b. Flag the unknown information using a question mark

Solving the Problem

1. Plan to solve the problem

   a. Find the total amount under the largest set of objects and write a "T" under the total
   b. Select an operation based on known and unknown information. (When the total is not known, add to get the total; when the total is known, subtract to find the part.)

(Continued)

(Continued)

2. Solve the problem

   a. Add or subtract
   b. Check to see if the answer makes sense
   c. Write the whole answer

SOURCE: Adapted from Jitendra, 2002.

Modifications for Operations in Elementary Math

While the tactics mentioned above address math word problems, we should not fall prey to the easy assumption that all mathematics difficulties after a certain age involve word problems. In fact, many lower elementary grade difficulties in mathematics involve work in complex operations such as multiplication, division, or fractions. The remainder of this chapter focuses on tactics to develop deep cognitive understanding of mathematical problems in various operations. For example, Lock (1996) describes several innovative modifications that can be used in the general education math class to assist both students who have difficulty in math and other learners. A list of simple modifications for learners who are challenged by math in the differentiated math class is presented below, followed by some more involved instructional modification ideas.

IDEAS FROM TEACHERS

Teaching Multiplication Tables

Teachers have discovered that for many children it is critical to start with easy work prior to moving into more difficult work (Lock, 1996). As an example of a skill progressing from easy to more difficult, consider instructions in times tables (multiplication math facts). Rather than teaching the times tables in order (1 × table; 2 × table; 3 × table; 4 × table, etc.), as is typically done, teachers can teach the multiplication facts from easy to more difficult by teaching the 1 × table and the 2 × table, followed by the 5 ×. This is easy because students can be taught (or may already know) the one and two levels, and may even be able to count by fives. Thus, the first tables taught tend to be confidence building and easy to memorize.

Next, one might teach the "doubles" (i.e., 3 × 3; 4 × 4; 5 × 5; 6 × 6; etc.). Next the teacher could produce a multiplication chart of math facts of all the multiplication tables from one through ten, and use that to illustrate how many facts in the new times tables the student already knows from the lower times tables. Thus, the times tables can be made easier by teaching from easy to more difficult.

Modification Options for the Differentiated Math Class

The following teaching tactics may be used in a differentiated math class (see Jitendra, 2002; Joseph & Hunter, 2001; Lock, 1996):

1. Structure new instruction for mathematics concepts as games between teams or as peer buddy activities. This helps involve students with interpersonal learning styles in the activity.

2. Stress "thinking through" the problem. Teachers should always follow up both correct answers and incorrect answers from students with a question about how the student arrived at that answer. As a modification of this idea, have students consult with a group of "peer colleagues" prior to answering the question, and have other students suggest alternate ways to get the answer.

3. Use cue cards for students involved in various types of math problems. The cue cards should present practical steps in problem implementation, and students should be taught how to discriminate when to use which set of cues. Post these around the room for immediate access.

4. Use graph paper to assist in lining up numbers and visualizing concepts.

5. Always have many counters or pictorial representations available in the classroom, and challenge students who get the correct answer to represent that problem solution for others in the class using these materials.

TEACHING EXPANDED NOTATION AND PARTIALING

Algorithms involve a combination of basic facts and more complex computations. Lock (1996) presented several ideas to give students alternatives to the typical method for solving simple problems in addition, subtraction, and multiplication. These include expanded notation and partial sums/products or partialing. Using these ideas in tear out groups can provide students with a novel, more interesting method of problem solution, and will help students unlock the deeper meanings of algorithms.

TEACHING TACTICS

EXPANDED NOTATION AND PARTIALING

Expanded notation involves identification of steps in transforming a complex math problem into a series of simpler math problems. This concept can be used in various operations such as addition and subtraction. Consider the problem 29 + 43 = _____. The expanded notation for this problem is presented below.

29	2 tens	and 9 ones
+ 43	+ 4 tens	and 3 ones

The problems would be completed as follows:

Add the ones and tens:	6 tens	+	12 ones
Regroup the ones, if necessary:	6 tens	+	(1 ten and 2 ones)

(Continued)

(Continued)

Put the tens together:	(6 tens and 1 ten)	+	2 ones
Write the tens & ones in simple way:	7	+	2
Write the answer:	72		

Partialing can assist some students in their approach to mathematics operations, and it leads to a deeper understanding of what the operations represent. A partial sum in addition would involve summing the ones column, summing the tens column, and then summing the sums, as follows:

$$37$$
$$+\ 64$$

First add the ones (7 + 4 = 11)
Next add the tens (30 + 60 = 90)
Next add the partial sums above (90 + 11 = 101)

An example of a partial product would be a bit more complicated, but it does have the advantage of demonstrating for the student what the multiplication process really involves. Consider the problem below. The partial product solution goes like this.

$$23$$
$$\times\ 12$$

First multiply each top digit by the 2
2 × 3 = 6
2 × 20 = 40

Next, multiply each top digit by the 1

10 × 3 = 30
10 × 20 = 200

Finally add the partial products

(6 + 40 + 30 + 200 = 276)

Note the use of the smaller multiplication sign (i.e., "×") in the ones place and the larger multiplication sign ("✕") in the tens place. This can help students remember that multiplying by tens results in much larger numbers.

SOURCE: Adapted from Lock, 1996.

IDEAS FROM TEACHERS

Rounding Numbers

Some students have difficulty grasping the concept of rounding off numbers. One teacher's innovative approach to teaching rounding involved a variation on the early video game called "Frogger." In that game, a frog was required to jump across a busy roadway and had to determine the best way to jump without being hit by a car. Of course, the frog could not jump the entire two lanes of the roadway in one jump, so it had to determine the safest way, and also determine when a car was coming from the left in the near lane or from the right in the far lane.

To develop a "frogger" course, teachers may place ten strips of tape across their floor, approximately one foot apart—this represents a "street" that the students must cross (the teacher will need ten feet of open floor space, but may use the rows between desks; this allows different students to play in different rows. All students must face in one direction, toward the front of the class). Have the student(s) begin to jump across the "street." Students may jump only when the teacher says "Jump." The teacher will then (at varied intervals) state that a car is coming in the left lane. At that point, other students in the class count down "five, four, three, two, one," representing the seconds until the car's arrival. Students in the track must either move or determine that the car is in the other lane. If a car comes from the left and the student is still in the left lane (i.e., if the student has jumped only five or fewer times), he or she must quickly jump back to the start line. However, if the student is in the right lane and a car comes from the left, the student may remain in that lane and wait for the teacher to call "jump" again. Using this "jumping to escape injury by car," one can usually illustrate the concept of rounding numbers.

PROCESS MNEMONICS
STRATEGIES TO TEACH COMPUTATION

One tactic to assist in operations and computation in the elementary classroom is based on process mnemonics (Higbee, 1987; Manolo, Bunnell, & Stillman, 2000). Mnemonics are schemes used for assisting with memory tasks, and process mnemonics stress the process of solving problems. Simple process mnemonics have been used as reminders of processes in a variety of subject areas (e.g., "'i' before an 'e' except after 'c' and when sounding like an 'a' as in neighbor and weigh"). However, little use has been made of process mnemonics in math instruction (Manolo et al., 2000).

Mnemonics are used in Japan to summarize the organization and the process of problem solving (Manolo, 1991; Manolo et al., 2000). Manolo and his coworkers (2000) hypothesized that since process mnemonics had been shown to be an effective teaching tool for students with normal abilities, it could hold promise for use with students who are struggling in math.

Implementation of Process Mnemonics

Process mnemonics utilizes representations of constructs in math that assist students with memory. In one research study, Manolo and others (2000) presented numbers as "warriors" and mathematical operations as situational military stories to teach the rules and procedures necessary for numerical addition, subtraction, multiplication, and division of whole numbers and decimals. Several example adaptations of this tactic are presented below.

PROCESS MNEMONICS FOR TEACHING DECIMALS

Subtraction: The process mnemonic for subtraction of whole numbers and decimal fractions tells students to imagine that the two numbers are different sets of warriors doing battle. The digit on each warrior denotes his strength. Warriors to the left of the decimal point are ranked, and those to the right of the decimal point are not ranked. To fight, the warriors must be lined up ranked against ranked and unranked against unranked in battle—this reminds the students to line up the decimal places prior to subtracting. The top group of warriors in the subtraction problem is designated the defenders and the bottom group is the attackers. The attackers can be recognized because they have their swords drawn (i.e., the minus sign in the problem).

$$
\begin{array}{ll}
24.6 & \text{defender} \\
-\,12.7 & \text{attacker} \\
\hline
\end{array}
$$

When subtracting, if the defender's strength in any column (i.e., the number in the top row) is less than the attacker's strength (the number in the same column on the bottom row), the defender has to be increased by ten in order to do battle. The consequence of this is that the next defender has his strength reduced by one. For example the problem above would become:

$$
\begin{array}{lcl}
24.6 & \text{changes into} & 23.6 + 10 \\
-\,12.7 & & -\,12.7 \\
\hline
\end{array}
$$

Students then solve for the answer: 11.9

Addition: Addition problems are presented as the warriors getting into a boat (Manolo, 1991; Manolo et al., 2000). The addition sign is the mast and the line below is the boat itself. Students should be taught that the warriors (numbers) to the left of the decimal point are ranked and those to the right are unranked, just as in the subtraction example above. They must always line up the lines of warriors ranked with ranked and unranked with unranked. If there is an unranked warrior lined up in the same column with a blank on the right of the decimal point, then the student should put a zero in that blank space, since a warrior with a rank of zero really doesn't matter and doesn't affect the outcome at all. In that type of situation the problem changes as follows:

$$
\begin{array}{lcl}
39.4 & & 39.40 \\
+\,12.45 & \text{becomes} & +\,12.45 \\
\hline
\end{array}
$$

If the numbers have no dots, then students could put dots to the right of the warrior farthest to the right, and then line up the warriors by using the dots. Finally, they would solve the problem.

$$
\begin{array}{lcl}
47 & & 47. \\
+\,9 & \text{becomes} & +\,9. \\
\hline
\end{array}
$$

Multiplication: Multiplication problems are presented as warriors at a meeting to exchange battle strategies (Manolo, 1991; Manolo et al., 2000). The warriors in the bottom set are the "experts," and are found next to the X or "times" sign. Each of these "X-perts" must meet each of the members of the group of warriors on the top row to teach them their "special battle techniques." For example, in the problem below, the "´-pert" 4 must meet with the 7, 5, 6, 8, and 3 of the top group. Students should be reminded to place ranked above ranked and unranked above unranked when they first copy down the problem. Multiplying the respective numbers and then writing the answers below the line produces the products of their planning meetings. The skills of the warriors become more specialized the farther left they are. Placing zeros whenever the student moves on to a more specialized warrior marks these specialized results.

$$
\begin{array}{r}
386.57 \\
\underline{\times\,23.4} \\
154628 \\
1159710 \\
\underline{7721400} \\
9035738
\end{array}
$$

Students should be shown how to count all the unranked warriors and then count that many places from the right to the left of the final answer to place the decimal point in the answer correctly. See the example below.

386.57 (In this problem, the student would count 3 unranked warriors)

$$
\begin{array}{r}
\underline{\times\,23.4} \\
154628 \\
1159710 \\
\underline{7721400}
\end{array}
$$

9035.738 (Thus, the 3 unranked warriors mean that the student should place the decimal between the 5 and 7 in the answer.)

Division: In division, the students are told to imagine the warriors standing in front of a rack of various pieces of armor (Manolo, 1991; Manolo et al., 2000). Each warrior is trying on a set of armor inside the cupboard, and the cupboard is represented by the long division symbol itself or $\overline{)}$. However, only ranked warriors may try on armor, so if the divisor has a dot (or a decimal), the dot must be moved all the way to the right. Also, the dot in the cupboard must be shifted the same number of places to the right. Thus, division problems are changed as indicated below.

$.08\overline{)34.26}$ becomes $08\overline{)3426}$ with all the decimals shifted two spots to the right.

(Continued)

(Continued)

Additional pieces of armor can be added to the rack if there is not enough armor already in the cupboard to shift the decimal the number of spaces needed. Students should be told that a decimal above the cupboard separates "expensive" armor from "inexpensive" armor. The warrior tries on the first piece or armor (in this problem, the size of that piece of armor is 3) and finds that it is too small to fit a big warrior (who in this problem is size 8). Therefore the warrior gets the next piece also, and the size now becomes 34. To tell how well the armor fits, the students should use a multiplication chart to look under the warrior's size (8) and go down that row in the table to find the size of armor closest to size 34 but not more than 34. Students should write the "measure of fit" below the armor piece in the question, then go across the table to find the number of times the warrior fitted the armor (in this example, it is 4).

Students should be told to write that number above the armor size in the cupboard, above the second digit in 34. At that point the student will have written: $08\overline{)3426}$.

To find out how much of the armor was not used, students should subtract the "measure of fit" from the pieces of armor being tried on. This leftover number (in this case, 2) should be checked to make sure it is not larger than the size of the warrior. The next piece of armor is then brought down from the cupboard and the warrior tries it on, looking for the "measure of fit" once again. This process is repeated until the warrior has tried on each piece of armor.

SOURCE: Adapted from Manolo, 1991; Manolo et al., 2000.

RESEARCH SUPPORT

Various research has shown that process mnemonics such as this is very effective for students with difficulties in math (Higbee, 1987; Manolo, 1991; Manolo et al., 2000). This tactic increases students' motivation in that the use of "warriors" makes math operations seem similar to many of the movies and video games that are so popular today. The metaphors involving warriors and their battles facilitate better retrieval of correct procedures.

Another reason why process mnemonics is so effective is that this tactic actively engages numerous fundamental mental principles of learning and memory, including organization of the constructs, association with well-understood concepts (e.g., warriors have enemies and battles), attention, and visualization. Higbee (1987) also suggests that process mnemonics provides structure that makes better sense to students. It uses concrete associations to link abstract symbols into a cohesive combination of relevance. For these reasons, teachers moving into differentiated math classes should consider using this innovative tactic for either tear out or mainline instructional groups.

WHAT'S NEXT?

In the last several chapters we have explored the transition from both hard reality math (e.g., the CSA approach) and a series of more advanced abstract, cognitively based instructional approaches for the lower elementary grades. Next, we turn to more cognitively based learning strategies for word problems in the upper elementary and middle school grades.

Web Site Review: SuperKids

The SuperKids Web site can be extremely useful to teachers in the elementary grades. It is one of the busiest on the World Wide Web because so many teachers, parents, and kids use it. The site allows teachers to create their own printable worksheets in a variety of areas, including operations (with both positive and negative integers), fractions (proper and improper), and rounding off. There is no mechanism for generation of answer sheets, so teachers (or students) will have to complete the problems (this could be a great tear out activity for one of the small groups in your differentiated math class).

www.superkids.com

Differentiating for Elementary Word Problem Solving

Strategies and tactics described in this chapter include the following:

- The Brain Research Basis for Metacognitive Instruction
- Read, Imagine, Decide and Do Tactic
- Steps for Implementing Learning Strategies
- The STAR Tactic
- The SQRQCQ Tactic
- Schema-Based Instruction

THE BRAIN RESEARCH BASIS FOR METACOGNITIVE THEORY AND TACTICS

Initially, there seems to be considerable overlap between the several types of guided cognitive inquiry methods described in the last chapter and the learning strategies approaches described below. These strategies and tactics all are directed toward the development of a deeper conceptual understanding of mathematics, as recommended by the NCTM standards (National Council of Teachers of Mathematics [NCTM], 2000). The metacognitive tactics described in this chapter, however, are not based in constructivist theory, as were the tactics described previously. Rather, these are founded on metacognitive theories of learning, an instructional approach that has become a dominant influence in educational psychology over recent decades (Jones, Wilson, & Bhojwani, 1997).

Metacognition literally means "thinking about thinking"; it is also defined as planning and monitoring how one performs a task. Metacognitive theory evolved in the 1970s and 1980s, and represents a significant change from earlier behaviorally based theories of learning. Metacognitive theory stipulates that

In metacognitive instruction, students are taught to specifically plan their thinking and subsequently monitor their own performance of those steps.

the thinking processes, which behavioral psychologists had always considered unobservable and therefore unimportant, are the basis for problem completion.

An example can help illustrate this point. Even in the simplest math problems a series of steps must be done sequentially in order to arrive at the correct answer. Consider the problem below:

$$45$$
$$\underline{+87}$$

At a minimum, this problem requires a student to:

1. Add the digits in the ones column (to get the sum of 12).

2. Write the digit "2" under the ones column.

3. Write the digit "1" at the top of the tens column.

4. Add the three digits in the tens column (to get the sum of 13).

5. Write both digits of that sum below the problem.

Of course, this series of sequenced steps can be difficult for students struggling in math; in particular, students with learning disabilities have difficulty with organization and planning tasks such as this. Thus, specification of these steps for the student allows the student to "think about his or her thinking" in solving the problem and in monitoring his or her performance.

More recently, brain research has shown that students use a different part of their brain to monitor their own steps toward problem completion than they use when actually doing the math problem (Sousa, 2001). While much mathematics thinking seems to be based in the right hemisphere and the visual cortex, much of the metacognitive thought is based in the forebrain areas of the left hemisphere of the cerebrum. Thus, for the problem above, the metacognitive thought—that is, the planning and monitoring of the steps toward problem completion—takes place in a different region of the brain than the actual addition functions. In doing math problem, students use their forebrain to "plan"

Again, metacognitive theory compliments the NCTM (2000) standards, because application of these metacognitive strategies is aimed at developing a deeper understanding of the constructs in mathematics as math is applied to real-world problems.

the steps and use other brain areas to conduct the actual calculations. If we as math teachers can teach explicitly the steps that a student must engage in to complete a math problem, that student will be better able to plan the steps in the problem and to monitor his or her progress in that problem. This will lead to higher math achievement.

Thus, this brain research has become the basis for metacognitive instruction. Sometimes this approach is referred to as learning strategies instruction, but regardless of the terminology used, the emphasis is on helping the student think through the problem conceptually.

Using metacognitive theory, a number of researchers have developed specific learning strategies or tactics that specify the steps that a student should complete in working on a problem (Woodward & Montague, 2002). These steps are typically represented by an acronym and are often committed to memory by the students. Other strategies are not identified by an acronym, but do represent an attempt to have students think through the math problems more deeply. There are some learning strategies that involve movement for memorization of definitions (see the example below on teaching metric measurement).

IDEAS FROM TEACHERS

Metric Measurement

This tactic involves a Simon-Says type of game and movement activity for teaching the basics of linear metric measurements. Rather than the acronyms used in traditional learning strategies, students are taught physical movements that represent metric measurements. Teachers may wish to use this tactic with younger students as a variation on Simon-Says types games by teaching the class movements associated with various distance measurements. When students hear the word *centimeter,* they should hold up a distance approximating a centimeter using the thumb and forefinger of one hand. When they hear the term *decimeter,* they should spread those fingers apart approximately 10 centimeters, or one decimeter. Next, for the term *meter,* the class should use two hands and hold them at arm's length to indicate one meter. Finally, when they hear the term *kilometer,* they should be told to drop their hands to their sides while the teacher explains that a kilometer is so large that it cannot be shown by using the human body.

First, the teacher should drill the class in those distances in order, saying something like, "Simon says, show me a centimeter." By scanning the class, the teacher can identify students out loud who have it correct, saying something like, "Thomas has it just right!" The other kids would then take a look at the distance shown by Thomas and emulate his movement. Thus this activity is self-correcting. Next the teacher would say, "Simon says, show me a decimeter," followed by a meter and kilometer. After repeating this several times, the teacher could say, "Now, I'm going to mix them up a little." In a one- to two-week unit on metric measurements, this activity could be repeated each day, until the basics of metric measurements are learned. For older students, the teacher may wish to drop the Simon-Says aspect and merely tell the class to, "Show me a decimeter," kilometer, and so on. Students will learn these metric distances through the learning strategy of movement.

LEARNING STRATEGIES FOR WORD PROBLEMS

Much of the metacognitive research on mathematics has concentrated on students' understandings of word problems, and word problems are an area with which many students struggle. Teachers in differentiated classrooms should have a variety of these tactics at their disposal, since these can be assigned to different tear out groups as problem-solving strategies. Several are presented below.

The RIDD Tactic: Read, Imagine, Decide and Do Tactic

The *Read, Imagine, Decide and Do Tactic* (*RIDD:* Jackson, 2002) uses imagery to help students transform new information into meaningful visual, auditory, and kinesthetic units. In using this tactic, new material is transformed into a student's own mental database, which makes learning more efficient. RIDD was first developed to aid students reading math word problems as well as directions within those problems, and has been used for students who were struggling in math across the grade levels. Moreover, this strategy is easily modeled for the class and thus less time is taken away from mathematics instruction to teach the tactic itself. Finally, some students view only the answer as important in math, so application of this strategy can teach these students that the process of doing the problem is an important consideration also. In short, there are a variety of reasons for the differentiated class to invest in this learning strategy.

Implementation of RIDD

The RIDD strategy, like many learning strategies, involves the use of an acronym, which specifies four metacognitive steps for the child to complete.

Read the Problem: The R in RIDD stands for "Read the passage from beginning to end." Students who are struggling in math tend to read a single line of text or a phrase suggestive of one operation and then stop rather than finish at the punctuation mark. Further, these students will also sometimes stop at an unknown word in the text, and this leads to incomplete understanding and incorrect answers. Consequently, this tactic involves teaching students to substitute a simple word, name, or nonsense word for the difficult word, and then to "keep on reading." Teaching students to substitute "their designated word" for unknown words aids in the release of memory processing resources and allows students to continue their process of constructing meaning from text. Such substitutions should even be made for long numbers in the text on the first reading. Then the student should be encouraged to read the problem again. In teaching this tactic, teachers should read a problem aloud using several substitutions and thus model the strategy. Students must be aware of why the teacher is substituting words.

R	Read the Problem
I	Imagine the Problem
D	Decide What to Do
D	Do the Work

Imagine the Problem: Step 2 of RIDD is represented by an I, and encourages students to "Imagine the problem." RIDD's use of imagery helps students to transform new information into meaningful visual, auditory, and kinesthetic formats. Also, this imagery process activates various areas of the child's brain and involves more cognitive resources in problem solution. The new conceptual material in the problem is then readily stored in the student's own knowledge base. The Imagine step serves two metacognitive purposes: First, it helps students focus on concepts or operations in the problem, and second, it aids students in monitoring their performance of the problem.

Decide What to Do. The first D in RIDD stands for "Decide how to do the problem." Students decide what to do to solve a problem by mentally reviewing what they comprehend from the text and the visual imagery they created for the problem. For young learners, the Decide step may be facilitated by teacher questioning to guide students in deciding what procedures to choose to solve the problem.

Note at this point how this tactic involves a number of techniques that have been discussed previously, such as use of imagery and cognitive guiding questions. This tactic pulls together these highly effective teaching tactics into one overall strategy, making this an excellent choice for many students in mainline instruction in the differentiated math class. Teachers may further involve those students by telling them that the mainline instructional group is going to learn a tactic that the tear out groups are not going to learn! This makes the mainline instructional group a more interesting place to be.

Do the Work: The final step is represented by the second D in RIDD and stands for "Do the work." Many students who struggle with word problems have a habit of reading through the problem only until they encounter the first suggested operation, and they then stop reading and begin the operation. Of course, this leads to errors, so the RIDD tactic emphasizes planning in several steps prior to doing any work. When beginning this final step, students use what they have already visualized and decisions they have already made about solving the problem in order to complete the work.

Students often indicate that they like RIDD because this final step is the only step in which they "do any work." As teachers implement this tactic they will sometimes hear students voice such thoughts. Of course, this indicates that students do not recognize that the metacognitive processes in the first three steps are part of the whole problem-solving process. Using RIDD helps students realize that there are other steps involved between reading a problem and doing the math.

Teaching Through Learning Strategies

There is considerable difference between knowing a learning strategy acronym and successful use of a learning strategy in the differentiated class. RIDD, like all learning strategies, is taught in several lessons over several weeks, and should become the basis for students' approach to all word problems. While various learning strategy theorists provide different guidelines for teaching a learning strategy, the steps presented below are common to the various learning strategy procedures and should be used with all of the learning strategies presented in this chapter. Further, for all learning strategy instruction it is critically important that the strategy to be learned is practiced repeatedly each day, until the strategy itself is memorized and therefore available for immediate use by the student.

TEACHING A LEARNING STRATEGY

1.   Explain the strategy and what it can be used for with some initial guided practice. Teach students to identify problems for which the strategy is appropriate and problems for which it is inappropriate. Make a poster of the strategy steps and keep it in front of the class.

2.   Explain the differences between spoken language and thought. Be sure that students understand that strategies are ways of thinking that can assist them in solving mathematical problems for the rest of their lives. This makes the strategy valuable to students and increases their motivation to invest themselves in the strategy.

3.   Introduce the strategy steps one at a time. Model each step separately and in combination with other steps. Reinforce each step and practice each step over a period of several days. Explicitly teach students to memorize the steps, to recognize the steps, and to identify the activities done in each step. Work with the students until each develops automaticity in strategy implementation.

4.   Use direct instruction (as described in Chapter 2) to teach the steps themselves. Once the students say and write the steps independently, they can begin to use them to solve problems.

5.   Aim for wide application and generalization to other problems. Once a strategy is learned, students should be provided with opportunities to practice the strategy daily for a period of time.

The Star Tactic

Another strategy that enables students to complete word problems is the STAR tactic (Gagnon & Maccini, 2001; Maccini & Hughes, 2000). The STAR tactic emphasizes the translation of the word problem into a meaningful mathematical equation, enabling the student to think through the problem prior to attempting problem completion. This strategy builds on the concept discussed previously of concrete, representational, abstract instruction. Although both manipulatives and representational imagery are used in this process, the emphasis here is on linguistic translation of the word problem into an equation. Thus, in contrast to the RIDD strategy above, the STAR strategy is primarily a language-based linguistic tactic that would be appropriate for students with a multiple intelligence strength in linguistic skills. The steps in the STAR strategy are presented below.

S   Search the word problem
T   Translate the problem
A   Answer the problem
R   Review the solution

The STAR Learning Tactic

Search the word problem

1. Read the problem carefully.

2. Ask, "What do I know, and what do I need to find?"

3. Write down the facts.

Translate the words into an equation in picture form

1. Choose a variable to solve for.

2. Identify the operations necessary (using cue words).

3. If possible, represent the problem with counters/manipulatives.

4. Draw a picture of the equation, including known facts and operations.

Answer the problem

1. Perform the necessary operations, solving for the unknowns.

Review the solution

1. Reread the problem

2. Ask, "Does the answer make sense? Why or why not?"

3. Check the answer.

SOURCE: Adapted from Gagnon & Maccini, 2001.

For example, for students with a strength in visual/spatial intelligence the RIDD visualization tactic would be a good choice, whereas STAR would be the appropriate selection for students with a linguistic strength. Of course, as a teacher moves into learning strategy instruction, it is possible to present too many options for students and thus to confuse the issues associated with word problems. Therefore, when teachers note that certain learning strategies are intended to serve the same function, the teacher should select only one of these for presentation to a struggling student.

> In the differentiated classroom, the math teacher should have as many instructional options as possible and should selectively target these instructional ideas to different students, based on the students' multiple intelligence strengths.

With that caution in mind, using different strategies for different members of the class in the differentiated math class can be a very effective tear out tactic. Again, in order to offer a wide diversity in the tactics and strategies used in the differentiated math class, teachers should have a variety of tactics at their disposal for use with various groups of students in the class. Presented below is one additional learning strategy for word problems, after which we will look at several other metacognitive approaches.

The SQRQCQ Tactic

Many mathematics concepts, in particular word problems, are taught by having the students read the problem. Therefore, a student's reading skills can directly hinder his or her achievement in mathematics. Of course teachers in all subjects must emphasize reading, but the skills associated with reading a word problem—where one term can change the entire meaning of the problem—are a bit more demanding than reading a passage in history or science. In fact, some students may have a strength in mathematics that is not reflected in their math grades because they are unable to read and comprehend the directions or the words necessary to perform the mathematic functions in the word problem. Therefore, teachers of mathematics must also teach reading, and one way to do this is to provide students with a graphic organizer that will assist them in seeing concepts and operations in the problem.

Barton, Heidema, and Jordan (2002) proposed a possible strategy to assist in reading the text of a word problem. The strategy is called the SQRQCQ method. Like the RIDD strategy discussed previously, this strategy is intended to assist students with thinking through exactly what the problem is and how they might begin to solve it. The steps are presented below.

Survey: Read the problem quickly to get a general understanding of it.

Question: Ask what information the problem requires.

Read: Reread the problem to identify relevant information, facts, and details needed to solve it.

Question: Ask what must be done to solve the problem: "What operations must be performed and in what order?"

Compute: Do the computations and compute a solution.

Question: Ask whether the solution process seems correct and the answer reasonable.

In several ways, this tactic is a bit more detailed than the RIDD tactic described above. For example, in this tactic the student is explicitly told, in the third step, to reread the problem. Also, the order of operations is stressed in the question step. Finally, this tactic, like all learning tactics, should be taught using the guidelines for teaching learning strategies presented above.

Web Site Review: Word Problems

Many math Web sites include activities for only the lower grades, and it seems finding appropriate sites for work on word problems is difficult. The EdHelper does include fairly extensive options for developing and/or downloading many worksheets on word problems. Other advanced mathematics topics are also included, such as: the metric system, quadratic equations, exponents, irrational numbers, polynomials, and more. This is a subscription Web site, but nonmembers can download many sample worksheets in a wide variety of areas for elementary and secondary mathematics.

www.edhelper.com

THE SCHEMA-BASED MATH STRATEGY

Students who struggle with math may face increasing difficulties as word problems become more sophisticated. For example, some complex problems involve mathematics operations to derive information that is used in subsequent operations to solve for the answer. The simple schema-based tactic initially described in Chapter 4 offers a learning strategy that is not represented by an acronym, but nevertheless can assist with increasingly complex math problems (Goldman, 1989; Jitendra, Hoff, & Beck, 1999). Even for the complex word problems that are often found in the upper elementary grades—problems that involve multiple operations—students can be taught to map critical features of math word problems into schematic diagrams as well as identify and solve for missing information (Goldman, 1989; Jitendra, 2002).

Schema-based instruction is defined by the use of schematic diagrams, and the diagrams presented in the previous chapter can be used with increasingly complex problems. Thus, schema-based instruction for higher level math involves the following:

1. Instruction in recognition of the various schemas presented in complex word problems,

2. Identification of the primary question posed by the word problem, and

3. Identification of any secondary schema that may be required.

The various types of schemas for simple word problems were presented in Chapter 4 (change schema, group schema, and comparison schema). To translate this into a more advanced instructional tactic we must consider two things. First, guidelines on teaching students to recognize various schemas in word problems are presented. Next, suggestions for using the schema-based instructional tactic for two-step word problems are given (Goldman, 1989; Jitendra, 2002).

Phases in Schema-Based Instruction

Initially, as discussed in the last chapter, students are provided schematic diagrams, and their task is to "fill them in" during their reading and solving of a word problem. You may recall that the diagrams for simple schemas were presented in the last chapter, so these will not be presented again here.

As students become more advanced, they should be taught to distinguish between various schemas and eventually to develop diagrams themselves. Thus, students will learn how to identify and map problem elements onto the schema diagrams after teacher demonstration and facilitative questioning help them identify critical elements. The phases of instruction focus on finding specific information in the text of a word problem, and subsequently translating this information into a schematic map. This process involves a number of steps (Goldman, 1989; Jitendra, 2002), which are presented below.

Distinguishing the Features of Various Schemas

First, teach the students how to distinguish the features of each problem type described in Chapter 4, focusing on problems that do not have any missing information. Students should be taught how to map features of the story with the help of explicit and overt modeling. Teachers should initially provide schema diagrams, then gradually wean students from them so that students eventually develop their own diagrams. Also, teachers must encourage frequent student exchanges to help all students identify the crucial elements of the word problem and map them on the schema diagrams. Teachers of differentiated classes should consider using a peer tutoring approach for this step, since students can use their interpersonal skills and generally will master this technique when it is demonstrated by their peers.

Teaching Change Problems

The purpose of this step is to emphasize the change schema problems, those in which students find the total amount by focusing on specific information in the text and using either addition or subtraction. Students should be taught that "change" problems start with a beginning set where objects and their respective values are defined. Next, a "change" occurs that causes the beginning set to change—by either adding or subtracting—into the ending set. Students should also be taught to examine the semantics of the problem, as well as to search for cue words in the text. In the following story problem a change occurs.

> Marty had 31 marbles on Friday. He lost 7 of them when he went to school one morning. How many does Marty have when he arrives at school?

The ending set here is less than the beginning set because Marty "lost" some of his marbles. The "change" resulted in fewer marbles at the end, and thus, change problems are time dependent. Students should begin to see that the beginning set number and ending set number cannot both be accurate at the same time because a "change" occurred in the problem. Students eventually should be able to recognize that in change problems where the problem ends up with more than at the beginning, the ending amount represents the total amount or the highest number in the problem. If the problem ends with less, however, the beginning amount to be used in the problem solution is the higher number of the two.

Teaching Group Problems

In "group" problems, time does not affect values like it does in "change" problems. In group problems, the smaller groups are combined to form a larger group or total set. In some cases, the total set provides the answer to the primary question in the problem, but in other cases one is solving to identify one of the smaller sets. Consider this example:

> Maryanne has 50 flowers in her flowerbeds. Of these, 28 are daffodils and the remaining are pansies. How many pansies does she have?

As you can see, "group" problem types involve the understanding of parts of a whole. They emphasize common attributes, flowers in this case, and distinctions within that broader group (pansies vs. daffodils). Students should come to understand that the whole is equal to the sum of its parts in "group" problems. Once students have the concept and have identified the missing information, they can solve for the correct answer.

Teaching Comparison Problems

"More than" and "less than" concepts are the focus of all comparison schema problems. Thus, in "comparison" problems, students should be taught to focus on two sets: one of smaller and another of larger value. Students should learn to identify one set as the comparison set and one set as the referent set. Consider this problem:

> Thomas has 46 baseball cards and William has 63. How many more cards does William have than Thomas?

Here the referent set is 63, and the comparison set is 46. It is critical for students to learn to identify the difference in value by comparing the two sets. This determination is made by evaluating the difference statement (using cue words and concepts such as *more than*) from the word problem.

Teaching Decision Rules

There are several rules for identification of the correct operations to be used in schema-based problem solving. For example, students should be taught to determine the correct operation for problem solving by determining whether or not the unknown value is the total (or the larger) set in the problem. Next, students should be taught that in a "change" problem, if the problem results in more, then the ending amount is the total, but if the problem ends up with less, then the beginning amount is the total. In "group" problems, the larger group is always the total. In "compare" problems, students must determine the total by examining the difference statement. Teach students that if the total is known, they subtract to find the missing amount. If the total is unknown, they must add to determine the total. These guidelines are summed up in the graphic of decision rules presented below. Teachers should consider developing a large poster of this as an organizer for students to be displayed at the front of the room.

TEACHING TACTICS

DECISION RULES IN SCHEMA-BASED INSTRUCTION

Finding the Total Quantity

1. Change Problems

    If the problem ends with more than it started with, the ending set is the total. If the problem ends up with less than it started with, then the beginning set is the total.

(Continued)

(Continued)

2. Group Problems

The larger set is always the total.

3. Comparison Problems

The larger set (compared or reference set) in the comparison of difference statement is the total.

Identifying the Operations

When the total is unknown, add to find the total.

When the total is known, subtract to find the unknowns.

SOURCE: Adapted from Jitendra, 2002.

Teaching Missing Elements

Next, the teacher should have the students review the problem schema and search for missing information. Teachers may lead demonstrations of various problems and encourage questioning to aid students in identifying and mapping the problem's critical elements onto schema diagrams. The students should search for and flag (i.e., highlight) the missing elements with a single question mark on the schema diagram. Have several students read the same problem, develop a schema diagram for it, and compare these, while the teacher clears up any misconceptions about critical and/or missing information.

Teaching Multischema Problems

After students master one-schema problems, they should be taught problems involving several schemas. For example, the following two-step problem involves both a change schema and a comparison schema. Students must determine the primary question and identify any missing information that will be necessary to solve for the answer to the primary question.

Paul had 34 apples. Peter gave him 7 more. Now Paul has 12 more apples than John. How many apples does John have?

Instruction on the use of schemas to solve two-step word problems focuses on backward chaining of two different schemas. Backward chaining is used to show the students how to first search for the unknowns in the problem and then solve for the final problem solution. Thus, backward chaining requires students to focus on the primary question asked and identify key facts in the surrounding text, as well as key unknowns that must be solved for prior to solving for the final answer. Students should be taught to write PA or "partial answer" by the answer to the secondary schema. They may use this notation in the primary schema to represent the missing information that will be provided by solving the secondary schema.

The change schema in the problem above involves addition (34 + 7) and then a comparison schema involving subtraction (41 – 12). Students would be taught to identify the primary problem question (i.e., the number of apples John has, which is provided via a comparison of apples owned by Paul and John) and the secondary problem or partial answer (PA: which represented the change problem concerning how many apples Paul has). Here is a diagram of this two-step problem.

Schema Diagram of a Two-Step Word Problem

Paul had 34 apples. Peter gave him 7 more. Now Paul has 12 more apples than John. How many apples does John have?

The Primary Schema: A Comparison Schema

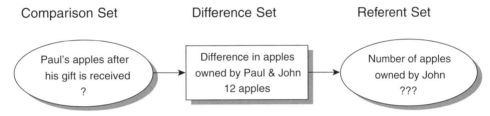

Problem Equation: ? – 12 = **???**

The Secondary Schema: A Change Schema

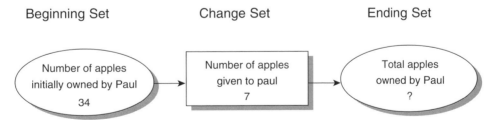

Problem Equation: 34 + 7 = ?   This is the PA (Partial answer) in the problem.

Note the use of the term *primary schema* to identify the ultimate answer to the problem question above. Also, using three question marks, in bold (**???**), identifies this unknown information as the final answer to the problem. The terms *secondary schema* and *PA* or *partial answer* as well as a single question mark (?) identify unknowns that must be solved for in order to answer the final problem. Teachers should explicitly teach these identification terms and markings in order to encourage students to specifically identify the unknowns in the problem as well as the final answer.

Schema diagrams can be modified to help students who have more difficulty with identifying and mapping the critical elements in math word problems. In the differentiated class, some of the diagram elements can be provided to some students on the schema diagrams; other students should develop their own diagrams and identify all of the elements themselves. Further, the number of elements already provided for certain students can be phased out as students become more adept at identifying the critical elements needed for their diagrams.

DIFFERENTIATED TEAR OUT ACTIVITIES FOR STORY PROBLEM SCHEMAS

Learning to master story problem schemas will be difficult for many students, since various word problems involve different degrees of complexity. For developing tear out activities in the differentiated math class, however, varying levels of complexity offer the opportunity to practice tiering the lessons. The teacher may challenge some tear out groups with a word problem with multiple schemas involved, whereas for other groups one-schema problems may be used. With four or five tear out groups working on different problems to determine the schema involved, the teacher will have ample opportunity to tier the work of the tear out groups to the students. This would be a good instructional activity for the second day on word problem schema. The lesson on that day should proceed as follows:

1. Orient the students to the idea of schemas, and remind them of the concepts discussed previously. Tell them, "Today, we will learn to identify schemas in word problems."

2. Specify the tear out groups of students and assign either single- or multiple-schema problems to those groups for analysis. Give the groups ten minutes to discuss the problem, make some notes on their work, and select the word problem schema for that problem.

3. Provide a map of all possible story problem schemas to assist groups of lower functioning students in identification of the schema in their problem.

4. The teacher should visit each group during the ten minutes in order to assure that the discussions are moving in the correct general direction.

5. Have each group report back to the class and identify the story schema involved in that word problem.

Research Basis

Results of a number of studies indicate that this schema instructional tactic can enable students who are struggling in math to learn to solve math word problems, including complex, two-step word problems (Goldman, 1989; Jitendra, 2002; Jitendra et al., 1998; Jitendra et al., 1999). Students in these studies who were having difficulties in math showed increases in math achievement for both single-schema and multiple-schema problems. Further, the use of the schema facilitated more correct choices of operations during problem solution. It also aided students to decrease calculation errors in two-step problems. The research has shown schema-based instruction to be effective from Grade 3 through high school. Clearly, teachers in the differentiated math class should consider using this tactic for struggling students across the grade levels.

IDEAS FROM TEACHERS

"One-Act Plays" for Word Problems

Having a tear-out group of students act out a word problem can be a highly effective and interesting tear out activity. Using any word problem as an example, the teacher could identify a tear out group and give them the assignment of acting out the word problem for the class later during the lesson. First, the problem should be written on the dry erase board so the class can look at the actual problem during its presentation. Next, the tear out group would plan and practice a brief one-act play to demonstrate the word problem and would present their play to the class. Finally, the students must be required to end the one-act play with a brief discussion of how the play showed the concepts to be demonstrated in the problem. This is a tiered assignment that will take some time and will be a challenge for some students, but for most heterogeneously selected tear out groups, 10 to 15 minutes should be enough time.

WHAT'S NEXT?

In addition to word problems and operations, teachers in elementary grades often must devise differentiated instructional ideas for some students who are progressing well in mathematics. Typically, this will involve moving students into more complex mathematics. The next chapter presents guidelines for working with learners in the higher grades who anticipate moving into secondary mathematics.

Differentiating for Higher Order Learning

The tactics and ideas presented in this chapter include the following:

- The Anchored Instructional Strategy
- The Teacher's Bank
- The PASS Learning Strategy
- Guidelines for Moving Into Secondary Math

WORKING TOWARD HIGHER ORDER THINKING

As students progress in mathematics into the upper elementary and middle school grades, the demands within the mathematics curriculum increase. For example, there is increasing emphasis on solving problems and on operations with fractions of all types, and there are more difficult constructs to master (Cawley, Parmar, Foley, Salmon, & Roy 2001). Also, with the recent emphasis on the National Council of Teachers of Mathematics (NCTM; 2000) standards, students are increasingly exposed to problems embedded in real-world scenarios. While many of the strategies and tactics presented previously continue to be quite effective in the higher grades, there are several additional tactics that should enhance the learning for all students in these differentiated math classes.

This chapter is intended to provide several strategy suggestions for students in the higher elementary grades. While several of the strategies presented in this chapter could have been presented in earlier chapters, they were reserved for this chapter in order to offer a progression of strategies based on the cognitive demands of the tasks. Whereas the tactics and strategies presented earlier have wide application in lower and middle grades, these tactics are more appropriate for more advanced mathematics in Grades 5 through 8. Keep in mind that many of the tactics presented previously are very appropriate for the higher grades as well, and teachers in Grades 5 through 8 wishing to differentiate their math class should review tactics and strategies from the entire text.

TEACHING STRATEGY: ANCHORED INSTRUCTION

As recommended in the NCTM (2000) standards, math instruction should be more grounded in real-world experiences and applied applications of mathematics to solve problems. No instructional procedure in math has emphasized the critical importance of real-world applications of math as much as the anchored instructional approach (Bottge & Hasselbring, 1993; Bottge, Heinrichs, Chan, & Serlin, 2001; Bottge, Heinrichs, Mehta, & Hung, 2002). In anchored instruction, applied mathematics from Grade 5 through Grade 8 is "made concrete" by using real-world story problems coupled with video vignettes. In the perspective of the proponents of anchored instruction, mathematics must be "anchored" in real-world problem solving, and this is accomplished most effectively by the creative use of video technology.

> In anchored instruction, video vignettes are presented to delineate the basic story scenario leading to the math problem, and the student is then challenged to solve various types of math problems based on these real-world video stories.

Anchored instruction originated at the Cognition and Learning Technology Center at Vanderbilt University in 1997 (Bottge et al., 2002). An early set of curriculum materials using video "anchors" (i.e., real-world math problem scenarios), called *The Adventures of Jasper Woodbury*, was published; it allows students to navigate videodiscs to solve geometry and algebra problems involving concepts such as distance, rate, and time. This curriculum is commercially available (see the information in the Web Site Review below).

Web Site Review: The Adventures of Jasper Woodbury

Information about this anchored instruction curriculum is available in two locations (see below). The first Web site is dedicated to providing information on the videodisc series for anchored instruction in math. Problems in this series are based on 12 video vignettes, each of which presents a series of real-world problem-solving challenges in a believable scenario that is highly interesting to middle school students. Sample story problems are presented on the Web site, along with photos from the video vignettes. This commercially available series concentrates on middle school math applications using basic algebra and geometry skills, and is currently in use in all 50 states. The series is intended for Grades 5 through 8 and is correlated with the standards of the NCTM (2002). Information on this series is available on the Internet:

http://peabody.vanderbilt.edu/projects/funded/jasper/jasperhome.html.

Additional information may also be obtained from the publisher:

www.erlbaum.com/jasper.html

The effect of using video anchors to present math problems can be both positive and quite profound for many students. Further, this enhancement of instruction is directly tied to the emerging insights from brain-compatible instruction. For example, Chapter 1 discussed the emotional brain and the key role played by emotional involvement with and motivation to solve the math problem. Without emotional involvement, students will tend to be less motivated to work on math. In particular, word problems as they are traditionally taught are often rather boring, and most students are not highly motivated to engage in solving the problems. Anchored instruction problems, however, are presented using video (specifically, videodiscs), and the student is directly and repeatedly shown the real-world context in which the problem is based. The video anchors used in anchored instruction are highly motivating and provide some "emotional intensity," leading students into increased involvement with the problem and toward problem solution. Students "get into" the story problems represented on the video, each of which presents a realistic scenario consisting of multiple subproblems in math (Bottge et al., 2002). Further, these subproblems can offer options for tiering math instruction and adapting the level of difficulty to various subgroups of students—thus differentiating the instruction. Clearly, this innovation offers a brain-compatible instructional tool for teaching word problems in math in the higher elementary grades.

In addition, researchers have now coupled use of these video anchors with subsequent applied tasks based on the video story in an effort to increasingly motivate students to successfully complete the series of math problems (Bottge et al., 2001; Bottge et al., 2002). Bottge and his coworkers (2001, 2002) refer to this as Enhanced Anchored Instruction or EAI. In short, by solving the math problems presented in the video examples, the students are concentrating on the mathematics, but that is followed by actually building something based on those mathematical solutions. That is quite motivating, even for the most reluctant math learner. For example, in one EAI teaching exercise, students were exposed to video anchors for between eight and ten days. Working in pairs, the students read building plans, using various mathematics to figure out the most effective use of building materials. This scenario was specifically constructed to involve a wide variety of math problems. The video anchor was, in and of itself, quite motivational, but the students' real motivation for this work was the opportunity to actually build their creation, a double skateboard ramp (Bottge et al., 2002).

> EAI makes use of challenging and motivating learning activities to link background knowledge to novel problems, computation skills to problem-solving strategies, and academic content to authentic tasks that have value beyond school. In so doing, EAI addresses the standards of authentic achievement, because students exhibit sustained effort to conceptualize the problems and sketch out ways to solve them (disciplined inquiry), organize and transform knowledge in new ways (construction of knowledge), and make products for use outside school (value beyond school). (Bottge et al., 2002)

In terms of differentiated instruction, the video anchors provide a variety of ways in which students may approach particular problems. With the guidance of both their teacher and their peer buddy—much of the anchored instruction research emphasizes the use of pairs of students working together—students begin to understand applied mathematics in much more concrete ways than in the traditional classroom. Also, for tear out groups, such videodisc-based instruction offers a wide variety of options for groups of students to work independently of the teacher.

While research has documented the efficacy of the anchored instructional approach (Bottge et al., 2001; Bottge et al., 2002; Woodward & Montague, 2002), this approach has not yet been widely implemented for several reasons (Woodward & Montague, 2002). First, this approach is very recent and is still in development. Next, development of a wider variety of videodisc curricula will be necessary prior to wide-scale implementation of these practices. Only a few curricula that employ the anchored instruction concept in mathematics are currently available, and only one of these is commercially available. Finally, increased validation of these practices for students across the ability spectrum is necessary, since most of the research has been undertaken with learners who are struggling in math.

However, several implications of this instructional approach are compelling. For example, in only a few years educators may use math curricula across the grade levels in which no math word problems are presented in written form to the students; rather, all problems beyond the math facts level could be presented using enhanced videodisc technology. In turn, this would effectively increase the motivation of most students to undertake efforts toward serious solutions to the problems presented.

Next, almost every educator has been challenged by a student asking, "How is this problem important to me?" In using anchored instruction, the "importance" or application of the problem is inherent in the video presentation of the problem. While this emphasis on practical, authentic problems from real-world situations will not satisfy all such questions, such challenges will be considerably reduced should we move to math instruction founded on the anchored instructional principles.

Finally, a shift in emphasis to anchored instruction will be realized only when appropriate curricula are widely available. Within the next several years, we may all expect the major publishing companies to produce video anchors, at first relatively rarely, but then more aggressively, so that within a ten-year period one may anticipate that almost all math instruction will shift to this concept of anchored instruction. As teachers are confronted with instructional demands for authenticity and practical applications of mathematics as stated in the NCTM (2000) standards, the anchored instruction strategy will certainly be one of the most important influences in the development of new mathematics curricula. Today, teachers should consider applications of the existing programs, such as the program mentioned above, and should embed anchored instruction within their curriculum whenever possible.

Prior to wholesale shifts to anchored instruction or EAI, however, several concerns must be addressed. Woodward and Montague (2002) raise the concern that lessons from anchored instruction may not generalize as well as conceptual lessons that are not as heavily based in context. Further, Woodward (2001) recently indicated that some of the problems considered socially relevant by those developing the video scenarios were not as relevant to 12- and 13-year-olds as was hoped. Thus several questions will have to be addressed prior to wholesale implementation of anchored instruction in math. Nevertheless, this approach will offer a plethora of tear out options to students in the differentiated class, and teachers moving into differentiated instruction should consider this instructional tactic as one option.

IDEAS FROM TEACHERS

Money Skills Using a Teacher's Bank

Anchoring instruction in video examples is merely one technique for teaching mathematics in an "applied" fashion. Teachers often use a "lower technology" idea for teaching monetary and banking skills. Many teachers in the middle and higher grades teach counting coins, making change, using paper bills, and even using checkbooks indirectly by opening a bank in their math class.

To begin, teachers should employ some type of play money: Monopoly money can be used. Each day teachers can pay students for the work they do, for appropriate behavior, or for any other accomplishment. In turn, once each week students may be offered the opportunity to spend their funds either on items from the teacher's store (e.g., pencils, paper, other items the teacher may wish to supply), or purchasing class privileges. Alternatively, teachers may simply begin by giving each student $100.00 in play money and have each choose the denominations in which he or she wants those funds (e.g., $10 notes, $20s, etc.). This will involve students in adding decimals, money management, and more. Students who have difficulty counting coins or bills can always request help from their peers.

Teachers should recognize that this play money has real value, since it can be used in the class to purchase things kids want. Teachers soon realize that they may have to deal with robbery, extortion, or any other real-world economic problem in the class, once the class begins using this money. However, with students able to buy privileges that they desire, or necessary and desirable items in class, they will be quite motivated to learn this system. The students will often ask for help from each other in adding up their funds (which teaches addition of decimal numbers). Of course, students must transact all purchases in correct amounts, and thus the very mechanism used for rewarding the class for good work is also an effective teaching tool. Additional ideas for this bank are nearly endless, and several ideas for differentiating this strategy into tiered instruction are presented below.

Differentiated Tear Out Ideas for Teaching Money and Banking

1. As soon as students master counting coins and bills, as well as adding/subtracting them correctly, teachers should develop a "checkbook" and teach them how to write checks (Jitendra & Nolet, 1995). This is particularly relevant in the upper elementary grades. Personally, in teaching students in Grade 8, I used a "class checkbook" and paid students for their work on every assignment. Each student was responsible for keeping a record of his or her earnings, and once each week the class "made a deposit" of the funds they had earned.

I frequently short-changed my students because I wanted to teach them to count their change themselves (particularly in real-world purchases). Also, students were responsible for personally adding up their earnings for Monday through Friday before they could purchase anything (e.g., educational game time, pencils, paper, old novels, or other things from my class store). Further, students had to get another student to check their work prior to receiving payment and entering the deposit in the checkbook. Finally, only after the weekly deposit was made could a student make a purchase. The check and check stub in Figure 6.1 allow for a "deposit" of funds each week and a one-check-per-week purchase.

2. Teachers may wish to use another student as the bank teller to check addition/subtraction of student's funds and/or checkbook deposits.

3. Use a student as the clerk if you operate a store in conjunction with your bank. This teaches some aspects of retailing and customer management, and also frees the teacher during that "store shopping time" to assist students with their math and their transactions.

4. In higher grades, an additional tiered version of this banking practice is to teach higher economic principles. For example, some teachers have sold "sickness insurance" that exempted students from makeup assignments for one- or two-day absences. Other teachers have paid interest on the amounts of savings in the checkbooks. Still others have established a "pretend stock market" by having students purchase stocks (using the real stock reports in the local papers) and track those stocks over time.

IDEAS FROM TEACHERS

A CSA Tactic for Pythagoras

This is a great tactic for a hands-on model of the Pythagorean theorem (i.e., the sum of the squares of the lengths of the sides of a right triangle is equal to the square of the

Balance Brought Forward	Student Name Here _____ Date _____
Deposit	Pay to the order of _____ $ _____
Total	_____ dollars
Check Amount	John Q. Schoolteacher Bank 123 School Street Yourtown, Yourstate 12345
Carry Forward	For _____ Signature _____

Figure 6.1   Check and Check Stub Register

length of the hypotenuse). I like presenting this because it demonstrates how a teacher can use CSA (concrete, semi-concrete, abstract) to develop a model of a higher mathematics concept. To demonstrate this theorem, use a tape measure and place a mark on a wall three feet from the corner. Next, go to the adjacent wall, measure four feet, and place a mark there. Present the theorem and challenge the students to figure out the length of the distance in a straight line (i.e., a line that does not follow a wall) between the marks. The distance should be exactly five feet, as predicted by the theorem.

THE PASS STRATEGY

PASS is both a relatively new theory of intelligence and a metacognitive strategy based on that theory. This strategy will effectively assist elementary students, middle school students, and older students in developing understanding of their own cognitive processes as those processes interact to solve a math problem. The theory is based on the growing understanding of intelligence, as founded within the emerging studies of brain structures (Das, Naglieri, & Kirby, 1994; Naglieri & Gottling, 1997; Naglieri & Johnson, 2000).

> The PASS strategy stresses thinking a problem through, using guiding questions and extensive self-reflection at various stages in problem completion.

Thus, PASS is intended to result in deep understanding of the algorithms, constructs, and problems under discussion, and is therefore consistent with the stated goals of the NCTM (2000) standards. The letters in the acronym PASS stand for

> **P Planning**
> **A Attention**
> **S Simultaneous**
> **S Successive**

The first mental function, *Planning*, is a process that is composed of the development of strategies and plans necessary to complete the problem at hand (Naglieri & Gottling, 1997; Naglieri & Johnson, 2000). This takes place predominately in the forebrain of the cerebrum and involves self-monitoring, self-regulation, and utilization of the processes involved in completing the task. As in many other learning strategies described in earlier chapters, this step enhances the students' thought processes and encourages the understanding that planning for problem solution is as important as actual problem solving.

The next mental function, *Attention*, refers to focused activity, resistance to distraction, and selective attention to the pertinent facts within the problem. Also, attention involves inhibition of irrelevant stimuli as well as an "appropriate level" of arousal in relation to the problem (e.g., what teacher has not experienced students who were either under- or overstimulated when a particular topic within a math problem was discussed?).

Next, the *Simultaneous* processing function takes place in the occipital-parietal areas of the brain. This process allows a person to deal with many pieces of information at one time and to arrange the information in groups for use in solving the problem (Naglieri & Gottling, 1997; Naglieri & Johnson, 2000).

Finally, the *Successive* mental function involves the integration of stimuli into a specific serial order. Thus this activity allows a person to work with information in a specific order or series; students may then determine what information presented is needed at each particular step in problem solving (Naglieri & Johnson, 2000).

As is obvious from the steps mentioned above, this learning strategy tends to be more holistic than the more specific strategies offered in the last chapter. Further, the steps in this strategy closely parallel the very mental processes that are utilized in solving complex problems (Das et al., 1994). Almost all students can benefit from personal, reflective consideration of their own mental processes in relation to the specific problem at hand. As described in Chapter 1, teachers in differentiated math classes are encouraged to specifically teach the multiple intelligences to students so that students can be equipped to consider their own mental functioning. Thus, the emphasis in PASS on the mental processes necessary to undertake a problem fits nicely within the differentiated class. Using PASS, students who are struggling in math are taught to think the problem through on the basis of their own mental processing skills.

Implementation of PASS

The implementation of the PASS strategy uses guided questioning and implementation based on a 30-minute math class (Naglieri & Gottling, 1997; Naglieri & Johnson, 2000). During the 30 minutes, students are required to complete math problems for the first ten minutes, hold a discussion for the next ten minutes, and complete math problems for the final ten minutes. These phases of PASS instruction are described below.

Initial Problem Work

First, students are given math worksheets that present math problems that have already been taught to the students in the tradition fashion. Thus, the students have, at a minimum, at least seen these types of problems before. The students are given ten minutes to complete as many problems correctly as possible, and are initially provided with no additional instruction. This period of work can be used to establish a pre-instruction score for the students.

Discussion

Next, the students hold a ten-minute discussion time. The teacher should not lead this discussion; rather, the students should, and the discussion may involve any topic at all. During this discussion time, student work is displayed anonymously on an overhead projector. In most cases, this is enough encouragement and results in students' discussing the work presented. If, after several 30-minute math periods over a number of days, the students are not discussing their personal approach to problem solving, the teacher should step in and lead the discussion in that direction (Naglieri & Gottling, 1997; Naglieri & Johnson, 2000). This "freedom to choose" to discuss math is viewed as essential during the initial days of instruction, since students who realize they make such a choice are much more likely to be "brain involved" in the subsequent discussions.

When the discussion does turn to problem-solving strategies for the work displayed on the overhead, the teacher should begin to participate more, using guided questions to focus on the students' mental processes during problem solving. The questions should challenge the students to do self-reflection in order to

1. See how each student completed the problems,

2. Have each student verbalize and discuss problem-solving ideas, and

3. Encourage each student to explain which methods worked well and which methods did not work as well.

Teachers can use a series of probing questions to assist students to jump-start their thinking as soon as the discussion turns to the problems on display. Some probes suggested by Naglieri and Gottling (1997) are listed below.

Early Probe Questions

1. Can anyone tell me anything about these problems?

2. Let's talk about how you did the worksheet.

3. Why did you do it that way?

4. How did you do the problems?

5. What could you have done to get more problems correct?

6. What did these problems teach you?

7. What else did you notice about how these problems were done?

8. What will you do next time?

9. I noticed that many of you did not do what you said was important. What do you think of that?

Remember that for this discussion the students have already been exposed to the types of problems on the worksheet but need assistance in planning their methods of problem solving. These probe questions are intended to allow the students to verbalize their individual thinking about the methods used. Thus, the guided questions and verbalization phase is the critical step in PASS.

Teachers can eventually turn the probing questions directly toward the planning, attention, simultaneous, and successive mental processes that are utilized in math. Again, having students discuss their own "brain thinking" during the math process is an excellent way to get students both involved and motivated. The questions below can serve as suggestions for this gradual transformation of the discussion.

Later Probe Questions

1. How did you decide what to pay attention to?

2. What numbers in the math problem did you have to use first? What numbers were used second? How did you decide when to use them?

3. Who can tell us how they thought through the problem before they started?

4. Does this problem have a partial answer?

5. Are there things that you have to remember when you do the final part of the problem? How can we "remember to remember" those things?

Unlike the earlier probe questions, these focus more directly on the mental process emphasized within the PASS strategy. By using the PASS tactic repeatedly over time, students should learn to focus more directly on their own mental processes while completing a math problem, and will thus become more cognitively engaged in problem solution.

Final Problem Work

Finally, after the students have discussed various problem-solving strategies, they are provided with an additional set of problems to complete. Students should be encouraged to implement some of the effective problem-solving ideas discussed previously, as well as to ask questions during this set of problems if they need a reminder for a particular strategy.

Results of Using PASS

Using PASS, students eventually figure out what method works best for them and the problems become easier. As new material is introduced, the students can discuss differences between the new problems and previous work. For some students the same solving strategy will work, while others may need to change their problem-solving strategies completely. The exchange of ideas allows students to discover possible ways to solve the current problems or new types of problems.

Eventually, students automatically try various ways to complete the problems on the worksheets and may begin to discuss problem-solving ideas with each other during the ten-minute work sessions. Teachers should not only allow but encourage this exchange! Students will start new worksheets using past successful problem-solving strategies. If these strategies do not work, they will use methods that other students have mentioned in the discussion periods.

Although some teachers are reluctant to offer free-ranging discussion time to students during the first few days of the PASS strategy—particularly given the time pressures of today's emphasis on standards and accountability—research has shown that these few sessions of time will not be a major concern. In the various research studies done to date, students generally take around three days before the ten-minute discussion started to revolve around various methods of completing the worksheets (Naglieri & Gottling, 1997; Naglieri & Johnson, 2000). Further, the freedom of choice that students are given is a critical motivating factor—they will pay more attention on subsequent days because of their choice to begin discussing the problem-solving strategies. Depending on the type of math problem, student discussions would eventually have planning strategy exchanges such as the following (for times tables work):

"I do the ones with the ones, zeros, and tens, they are easy."

"I do the fives too."

"I move my seat when I am distracted."

"I do the problems row by row."

"I like to do one problem from the top of the sheet, and one from the bottom row, since I like working toward the middle."

As these quotes attest, students will share both effective and noneffective strategies, and the teacher should encourage discussion of all strategies.

Suggested Uses for PASS

As is apparent above, the PASS instructional tactic can be used for almost any type of math operations problems and even for simple and complex word problems. Teachers could use this theory to improve students' basic addition and rote memory of certain facts. Further, using a large number of problems (since the students will engage in two ten-minute work periods each day) reduces the stress in math for some students. Students who are afraid to get a problem wrong will soon understand that the problems will be discussed as a class, and that the problem solving is more important than receiving a "good grade" during each work period.

> Students should be trusted to sort through the strategies to identify the ones that work and the ones that are not effective—this is a critical learning component for math, as stated in the NCTM (2000) standards.

This approach can also be used for math problems like multiplication and division. Students who use repetition of facts will probably memorize the facts more rapidly. Students are generally taught the multiplication facts in groups, and use of various memory strategies and ideas can be critical. For instance, to recall $7 \times 9 = 63$, a student might start with the easier fact of $7 \times 7 = 49$, and then "build up" to $7 \times 8 = 56$, and finally $7 \times 9 = 63$. When discussing this strategy, students will quickly discover that while this process works, it takes a much longer time to answer the problem than using automatic recall. PASS theory allows students to discuss these tactics among themselves with only minimal teacher guidance in the discussion.

In algebra, problems involve solving for "X" and often involve repetition of steps. PASS can assist in this higher level of metacognitive planning. Also, giving a student a worksheet that presents these steps over and over again will allow the student to recall the steps later. In geometry, PASS can be used to train the student in all of the various formulas. These formulas could be anything from the area of a triangle to the area of a rhombus. Of course, complex problems take more time, so the more complex the type of problems on the worksheet, the fewer completed problems should be expected during a ten-minute work session.

Finally, PASS may offer one area in which math instruction can become a broader vehicle for improved cognitive understandings. For example, the proponents of PASS suggest that these problem-solving approaches provide students with a problem-solving strategy that can be utilized in all areas of academic work and subsequently in various areas of life (Naglieri & Gottling, 1997; Naglieri & Johnson, 2000). Ideally, students will eventually form the habit of asking others how they approached particular problems, and of sharing their own problem-solving strategies.

Research Support for PASS

A variety of research studies have been done that support the use of the PASS strategy for instruction in math (Das et al., 1994; Naglieri & Gottling, 1997; Naglieri & Johnson, 2000). Most of these studies researched this tactic on students who were in either elementary or middle school; they also involved students with difficulties in math. The research consistently shows improvement in math achievement as a result of PASS. Further, students who were less adept at planning their problem-solving tactics typically demonstrated the greatest improvement. Students with high planning skills improved, but not as rapidly as the students with low planning skills. Thus, research has shown that PASS is effective for all students in the differentiated math class.

Of course, more research is needed on use of this tactic in a broader age range, but the promise of a "higher order" strategy that focuses students directly on the mental processes used in both simple and complex math problems is compelling. In the differentiated classroom this tactic is a must for the initial tear out students who are demanding a higher level involvement with the problems at hand, and the good news is that this tactic works for everyone in the math class!

MOVING ON UP! MATH INSTRUCTION GUIDELINES FOR SECONDARY LEARNERS

When the strategies and tactics presented up to this point in this text are employed in the differentiated math class as either tear out instructional options or for mainline instruction, teachers should be able to construct a variety of differentiated instructional activities for students with a wide range of abilities in every grade level. The array of activities, including CSA, learning strategies, scaffolding tactics, and many others, offer an exciting set of instructional choices for teachers to use. Further, continued use of these innovative tactics can assist in the gradual progression into higher level math in the secondary school.

Jones, Wilson, and Bhojwani (1997) provided some guidelines for how teachers may design practice activities that will be involving for middle school and secondary learners who have difficulty in math. In general, for learners who have difficulty in math the teacher's challenge is to present complex math in a way that does not embarrass the students, but that does include appropriate scaffolding to support the students' learning during the practice phases of instruction. This may involve many of the strategies presented in earlier chapters, such as use of representations of mathematical problems, concrete examples, scaffolding, guided questions, and process mnemonics.

These guiding principles, delineated by Jones and coworkers (1997) and modified for the differentiated classroom, are presented below. With these ideas in hand, and the plethora of tactics described previously, teachers should be able to construct a highly differentiated math class that increases success in math for all learners.

TEACHING TACTICS

DESIGNING MATH ACTIVITIES FOR MIDDLE SCHOOL AND SECONDARY LEARNERS

1. Avoid memory overload by assigning manageable amounts of practice work as skills are learned. Present the practice work in a variety of ways that are intended to involve as many of the multiple intelligences as possible over the course of an instructional unit. Let students know at the beginning of each instructional unit what the planned activities are and which multiple intelligences will be stressed, so that each student can anticipate an interesting learning experience when his or her intelligence strength is emphasized on a particular day within the unit.

2. Build retention by providing review within a day or so of the initial learning of difficult skills. Provide supervised practice to prevent students from practicing misconceptions and misrules. Use peer buddy plans to assist in practice. Employ novelty to assist in memory exercises, and process mnemonics activities whenever possible.

3. Reduce interference between concepts or applications of rules and strategies by separating practice opportunities until the discriminations between them are learned. After the discriminations are mastered, emphasize the decisions students must make in determining which concepts seem to conflict with each other.

4. Make new learning meaningful by relating the practice of subskills to the performance of the whole task. Discuss the whole task and subskills with the students, and have the students reflectively consider what they learned about mathematics.

5. Give credit for partial answers in two-step problems, and offer graphic representations of them.

6. Reduce processing demands by preteaching component skills of algorithms and strategies, and by teaching easier knowledge and skills before teaching difficult knowledge and skills.

7. Require fluent responses. Offer a variety of methods for presenting responses, such as oral, group work, written work, pictorial work, and so on.

8. Ensure that skills to be practiced can be completed independently with high levels of success before moving on to new skills. Use peers to do periodic review activities.

References

Allsopp, D. H. (1997). Using classwide peer tutoring to teach beginning algebra problem-solving skills in heterogeneous classroom. *Remedial and Special Education, 18*(6), 367–379.

Allsopp, D. H. (1999). Using modeling, manipulatives, and mnemonics with eighth grade math students. *Teaching Exceptional Children, 32*(2), 74–81.

Alsup, J. K. (2003). New classroom rules to promote preservice elementary teachers' mathematics learning education. *ChulaVista, 123*(3), 609–615.

Barton, M. L., Heidema, C., & Jordan, D. (2002). Teaching reading in mathematics and science. *Educational Leadership, 60*(3), 24–28.

Behrend, J. (2003). Learning-disabled students make sense of mathematics. *Teaching Children Mathematics, 9*(5), 269–274.

Bender, W. N. (1996). *Teaching students with mild disabilities.* Boston: Allyn & Bacon.

Bottge, B. A., & Hasselbring, T. (1993). A comparison of two approaches for teaching complex, authentic mathematics problems to adolescents in remedial math classes. *Exceptional Children, 59,* 545–556.

Bottge, B. A., Heinrichs, M., Chan, S., & Serlin, R. C. (2001). Anchoring adolescents' understanding of math concepts in rich problem-solving environments. *Remedial and Special Education, 22*(5), 299–314.

Bottge, B. A., Heinrichs, M., Mehta, Z. D., & Hung, Y. (2002). Weighing the benefits of anchored math instruction for students with disabilities in general education classes. *Journal of Special Education, 35*(4), 186–200.

Carpenter, T. P., Fennema, E., & Franke, M. L. (1996). Cognitively guided instruction: A knowledge base for reform in primary mathematics instruction. *Elementary School Journal, 97*(1), 3–20.

Cawley, J., Parmar, R., Foley, T., Salmon, S., & Roy, S. (2001). Arithmetic performance of students: Implications for standards and programming. *Exceptional Children, 67*(3), 311–328.

Checkley, K. (1999), Math in the early grades: Laying a foundation for later learning. *Association of School Curriculum Development.* Available online at www.ascd.org/readingroom/cupcake/1999/1sum.html

Das, J. P., Naglieri, J. A., & Kirby, J. R. (1994). *Assessment of cognitive processes: The PASS theory of intelligence.* New York: Allyn & Bacon.

Forsten, C., Grant, J., & Hollas, B. (2002). *Differentiated instruction: Different strategies for different learners.* Peterborough, NH: Crystal Springs Books.

Fuson, K. C., & Wearne, D. (1997). Children's conceptual structures for multi digit numbers and methods of multi digit addition and subtraction. *Journal of Research in Mathematics Education, 28*(2), 130–163.

Gagnon, J. C., & Maccini, P. (2001). Preparing students with disabilities in algebra. *Teaching Exceptional Children, 34*(1), 8–15.

Gardner, H. (1983). *Frames of mind.* New York: Basic Books.

Gardner, H. (1993). *Multiple intelligences: The theory in practice.* New York: Basic Books.

Geller, C. H., & Smith, K. S. (2002, October). *Improving the teaching of math: From textbook concepts to real-world applications.* Paper presented at the annual meeting of the Council for Learning Disabilities, Denver, CO.

Gersten, R., & Chard, D. (1999). Number sense: Rethinking arithmetic instruction for students with mathematical disabilities. *Journal of Special Education, 44,* 18–28.

Gersten, R., Chard, D., Baker, S., & Lee, D. (2002, October). *Instructional approaches for teaching mathematics to students with learning disabilities: Findings from a synthesis of experimental research.* Paper presented at the annual meeting of the Council for Learning Disabilities, Denver, CO.

Goldman, S. (1989). Strategy instruction in mathematics. *Learning Disability Quarterly, 12,* 43–55.

Greenwood, C. R., Delquadri, J. C., & Hall, R. V. (1989). Longitudinal effects of class-wide peer tutoring. *Journal of Educational Psychology, 81,* 371–383.

Griffin, S., Sarama, J., & Clements, D. (2003). Laying the foundation for computational fluency in early childhood. *Teaching Children Mathematics, 9*(6), 306–310.

Grobecker, B. (1999). Mathematics reform and learning differences. *Learning Disability Quarterly, 22*(1), 43–58.

Grobecker, B., & De Lisi, R. (2000). An investigation of spatial-geometrical understanding in students with learning disabilities. *Learning Disabilities Quarterly, 23*(2), 7–16.

Gurgasnus, S. (2004). Promote number sense. *Intervention in School and Clinic, 40*(1), 55–58.

Harniss, M. K., Carnine, D. W., Silbert, J., & Dixon, R. C. (2002). Effective strategies for teaching mathematics. In E. J. Kame'enui, D. W. Carnine, R. C. Dixon, D. C. Simmons, & M. D. Coyne (Eds.), *Effective teaching strategies that accommodate diverse learners.* Upper Saddle River, NJ: Merrill/Prentice Hall.

Harris, C. A., Miller, S. P., & Mercer, C. D. (1995). Teaching initial multiplication skills to students with disabilities in general education classrooms. *Learning Disabilities Research and Practice, 10*(3), 180–195.

Hearne, D., & Stone, S. (1995). Multiple intelligences and underachievement: Lessons from individuals with learning disabilities. *Journal of Learning Disabilities, 28*(7), 439–448.

Higbee, K. L. (1987). Process mnemonics: Principles, prospects, and problems. In M. A. McDaniel & M. Pressley (Eds.), *Imagery and related mnemonic processes: Theories, individual differences and applications* (pp. 407–427). New York: Springer.

Jackson, F. (2002). Crossing content: A strategy for students with learning disabilities. *Intervention in School and Clinic, 37*(5), 279–283.

Jitendra, A. (2002). Teaching students math problem-solving through graphic representations. *Teaching Exceptional Children, 34*(4), 34–38.

Jitendra, A. K., Griffin, C., McGoey, K., Cardill, C., Bhat, P., & Riley, T. (1998). Effects of mathematical word problem solving by students at risk or with mild disabilities. *Journal of Educational Research, 91,* 345–356.

Jitendra, A. K., Hoff, K., & Beck, M. M. (1999). Teaching middle school students with learning disabilities to solve word problems using a schema-based approach. *Remedial and Special Education, 20*(1), 50–64.

Jitendra, A., & Nolet, V. (1995). Teaching how to use a check register: Procedures for instruction selection and design. *Intervention in School and Clinic, 31*(1), 28–33.

Jitendra, A., & Xin, Y. P. (2002, October). *An analysis of problem solving instruction in third-grade mathematics textbooks: Adherence to instructional design principles and the NCTM standards.* Paper presented at the annual meeting of the Council for Learning Disabilities, Denver, CO.

Johnson, D. T. (2000). *Teaching mathematics to gifted students in a mixed-ability classroom.* ERIC Clearinghouse on Disabilities and Gifted Education. EC Digest, No. E594.

Jones, E. D., Wilson, R., & Bhojwani, S. (1997). Mathematics instruction for secondary students with learning disabilities. *Journal for Learning Disabilities, 30*(2), 151–163.

Jordan, L., Miller, M., & Mercer C. (1998). The effects of concrete to semi-concrete to abstract instruction in acquisition and retention of fraction concepts and skills. *Learning Disabilities: A Multidisciplinary Journal, 9*(3), 115–122.

Jordan, N. C., Levine, S. C., & Huttenlocher, J. (1995). Calculation abilities in young children with different patterns of cognitive functioning. *Journal of Learning Disabilities, 28*(1), 53–64.

Joseph, L. M., & Hunter, A. D. (2001). Differential application of cue card strategy for solving fraction problems: Exploring instructional utility of the cognitive assessment system. *Child Study Journal, 31*(2), 123–136.

Karp, K. S., & Voltz, D. L. (2000). Weaving mathematical instructional strategies into inclusive settings. *Intervention in School and Clinic, 35*(4), 206–215.

Katz, J., Mirenda, P., & Auerbach, S. (2002). Instructional strategies and educational outcomes for students with developmental disabilities in inclusive "multiple intelligences" and typical inclusive classrooms. *Research and Practice for Persons With Severe Disabilities, 27*(4), 227–238.

Koscinski, S., & Gast, D. (1993). Use of constant time delay in teaching multiplication facts to students with learning disabilities. *Journal of Learning Disabilities, 26*(8), 533–544, 567.

Larkin, M. J. (2001). Providing support for student independence through scaffolded instruction. *Teaching Exceptional Children, 34*(1), 30–35.

Lock, R. H. (1996). Adapting mathematics instruction in the general education classroom for students with mathematics disabilities. *LD Forum* (Winter). Electronic edition available at www.ldonline/ld_indepth/math_skills/adapt_cld.html

Maccini, P., & Gagnon, J. C. (2002). Perceptions and applications of NCTM standards by special and general education teachers. *Exceptional Children, 68*(3), 325–344.

Maccini, P., & Hughes, C. A. (2000). Effect of a problem solving strategy on the introductory algebra performance of secondary students with learning disabilities. *Learning Disabilities Research & Practice, 15*(1), 10–21.

Maccini, P., McNaughton, D., & Ruhl, K. L. (1999). Algebra instruction for students with learning disabilities: Implications from a research review. *Learning Disability Quarterly, 22*, 113–124.

Manolo, E. (1991). The incorporation of process mnemonic instruction in teaching computational skills: A case report on a mathematics learning disabled individual. *Focus on Learning Problems in Mathematics, 13*(4), 21–34.

Manolo, E., Bunnell, J. K., & Stillman, J. A. (2000). The use of process mnemonics in teaching students with mathematics learning disabilities. *Learning Disability Quarterly, 23*(2), 137–156.

Marsh, L. G., & Cooke, N. L. (1996). The effects of using manipulatives in teaching math problem solving to students with learning disabilities. *Learning Disabilities Research and Practice, 11*(1), 58–65.

Montague, M. (1997). Student perception, mathematical problem solving, and learning disabilities. *Remedial and Special Education, 18*(1), 46–53.

Mortweet, S. L., Utley, C. A., Walker, D., Dawson, H. L., Delquadri, J. C., Reddy, S. S., Greenwood, C. R., Hamilton, S., & Ledford, D. (1999). Classwide peer tutoring: Teaching students with mild mental retardation in inclusive classrooms. *Exceptional Children, 65*(4), 524–536.

Naglieri, J. A., & Gottling, S. H. (1997). Mathematics instruction and PASS cognitive processes: An intervention study. *Journal of Learning Disabilities, 30*(5), 513–520.

Naglieri, J. A., & Johnson, D. (2000). Effectiveness of a cognitive strategy intervention in improving arithmetic computation based on the PASS theory. *Journal of Learning Disabilities, 33*(6), 591–597.

National Council of Teachers of Mathematics. (2000). *Principles and standards for school mathematics.* Available online at http://standards.nctm.org/index.html

Schuster J. W., Stevens, K. B., & Doak, P. K. (1990). Using constant time delay to teach word definitions. *Journal of Special Education, 24,* 306–317.

Shaw-Jing, C., Stigler, J. W., & Woodward, J. A. (2000). The effects of physical materials on kindergartners' learning of number concepts. *Cognition & Instruction, 18*(3), 32–64.

Sousa, D. A. (2001). *How the special needs brain learns.* Thousand Oaks, CA: Corwin Press.

Stading, M., Williams, R. L., & McLaughlin, T. F. (1996). Effects of a copy, cover, and compare procedure on multiplication facts mastery with a third grade girl with learning disabilities in a home setting. *Education and Treatment of Children, 19,* 425–434.

Stern, C. (1949). *Children discover arithmetic.* New York, Harper.

Strauss, V. (2003, December 1). Trying to figure out why math is so hard for some. *Washington Post.*

Thompson, P. W. (1992). Notations, conventions, and constraints: Contributions to effective uses of concrete materials in elementary mathematics. *Journal for Research in Mathematics Education, 23*(2), 123–147.

Tomlinson, C. (1999). *The differentiated classroom: Responding to the needs of all learners.* Alexandria, VA: Association for Supervision and Curriculum Development.

Touchette, P. (1971). Transfer of stimulus control: Measuring the movement of transfer. *Journal of Experimental Analysis of Behavior, 15,* 347–354.

Whitenack, J. W., Knipping, N., Loesing, J., Kim, O. K., & Beetsma, A. (2002). Supporting first graders' development of number sense. *Teaching Children Mathematics, 9*(1), 26–33.

Wiggins, G., & McTighe, J. (1998). *Understanding by design.* Alexandria, VA: Association for Supervision and Curriculum Development.

Wirtz, R. (1981). *New beginnings.* Monterey, CA: Curriculum Development Associates.

Wolery, M., Bailey, D. B., & Sugai, G. M. (1988). *Effective teaching: Principles and procedures of applied behavior analysis with exceptional students.* Boston: Allyn & Bacon.

Wolery, M., Cybriwsky, C. A., Gast, D. L., & Boyle-Gast, K. (1991). Use of constant time delay and attentional responses with adolescents. *Exceptional Children, 57,* 462–473.

Woodward, J. (2001). Constructivism and the role of skills in mathematics instruction for academically at-risk secondary students. *Special Services in the Schools, 17*(1–2), 15–32.

Woodward, J., & Montague, M. (2002). Meeting the challenge of mathematics reform for students with LD. *Journal of Special Education, 36*(2), 89–102.

Index

A Workshop Facilitator's Guide

I n this facilitator's guide, I present my thoughts and suggestions for conducting workshops on the contents of this book. In each chapter section below, I have presented three components:

Major Points in the Chapter

General Discussion Questions

Workshop Activity Ideas

The goal in any workshop I conduct is to provide new instructional ideas, or variations on familiar ideas, and to involve the participants. Here, I informally share a variety of activities that should get the participants involved in various workshop activities. Of course, any workshop activity will be more or less effective depending on the audience, the setting, and the ability of the workshop provider to involve the participants meaningfully. Toward that end, a good set of innovative instructional ideas, a variety of small group activities, and a good sense of humor are all critical in workshop presentation. I sincerely hope these ideas can assist you.

CHAPTER 1: THE MATHEMATICAL BRAIN: DIFFERENTIATED INSTRUCTION AND MATHEMATICAL THINKING

Major Points in Chapter 1

To understand differentiated instruction in the math class, teachers need a firm grasp of two of the founding ideas that underlie differentiated instruction—multiple intelligences (MI) and brain-compatible instruction. Chapter 1 presents the current information on how the brain functions during math tasks, and while an in-depth understanding of brain physiology is not the goal, knowing that much mathematical thinking takes place in the visual cortex, the forebrain, and the parietal lobe can assist teachers in understanding that much of what we do in math involves metacognitive thinking, or "planning" of the math task. Further, having a grasp of how critical emotional involvement is in learning can help math teachers understand the importance of developing in their students an appreciation of mathematics rather than a fear of it. Finally, some understanding of the results of the research in recent decades on how the brain functions during mathematics will equip teachers to better interpret the later chapters of the book. Special attention should be given to the following points:

1. Describe the regions of the brain involved in math, and how the areas involved in reading skills may impact mathematics achievement.

2. Describe the issues involved in gender maturation within the brain, and how such gender differences may explain early learning differences.

3. Discuss the fact that only basic numeration is hardwired in the brain; thus most of math is dependent on learning.

4. Describe the priorities of our "emotional" brain. Relate the importance of emotion in learning to the fact that mathematics is often the subject that engenders fear in some students.

5. Discuss the human brain as a filter of information; this emphasizes the importance of novel, exciting learning activities as recommended by the differentiated instruction concept.

6. Discuss number sense. This allows children to make sense of numbers and may be as fundamental for math learning as phoneme instruction is for reading.

7. Multiple intelligences provide one mechanism for differentiating activities in the math class. Note several examples of the types of instructional activities that involve each of the eight intelligences noted in the chapter.

While the multiple intelligences concept is not new, the growing differentiated instruction movement has resulted in a reinvestment in the multiple intelligences concept. Teachers have for years been told to plan activities using multiple intelligences, and thus to address a variety of multiple intelligences in the classroom. The grid provided in this chapter can assist teachers in planning instructional units that do involve a variety of multiple intelligence activities, in each of three ways—concrete, representational, abstract.

The new mandate, however, is to teach students about their own learning strengths. This emphasis on multiple intelligences in the math class can assist students in thinking about how they may best learn particular content. In the math workshops I do, I continually refer to the multiple intelligences concept by inquiring, "Which of the multiple intelligences does that idea address?"

Finally, a number of teaching ideas are presented throughout the chapter, including several "Top Ten Lists." These should be reviewed. Also, because ideas for the development of number sense among children have not been presented in many math curricula to date, a variety of instructional ideas are presented.

General Discussion Questions

1. What ideas can we generate concerning how various multiple intelligences may be employed in a particular math lesson? Are there some intelligences that are more difficult to generate instructional ideas for? Have teachers share specific tactics they have used that focus on chanting, movement, or other activities that stress multiple intelligences.

2. Review the concept of number sense, and challenge teachers to write a three-sentence description of a learning task that would allow children to demonstrate that they have developed number sense. What are the indicators of children's understanding of number sense?

3. Describe the concept of teaching to "big ideas" in mathematics. The big ideas concept suggests that in any subject area there are ideas that cut through specific chapters, content areas, and grade levels. Have a discussion on what these big ideas may be in elementary mathematics. How do these big ideas relate to the brain's tendency to seek patterns in learning?

4. Describe ways to increase novelty in mathematics instruction. One idea is to use the rhythm of a popular song (the Clap, Clap, Slap Desk, Rest-rhythm of "We will, we will, rock you!"). Using that rhythm, chant the three's times tables ("Three times one is three; three times two is six; three times three is nine, . . ."). Have teachers generate and share other ideas. In almost any elementary school, many teachers are using certain songs, rhythms, or chants to teach various things. Take a few moments to share these among the faculty. Many of the "Ideas From Teachers" presented here came from teachers in various workshops.

5. Review the math curriculum used in the school district, and note how connections are made between previous lessons and today's lesson. Are appropriate scaffolds provided that relate today's task to previous tasks? Are all students' needs met by these activities, or are additional connections needed by some students?

6. Have the teachers discuss the sample activity on addition of positive and negative integers described at the end of the chapter. Provide a description of this movement activity and have teachers identify the multiple intelligences involved.

Workshop Activity Ideas

1. Hold an Informal Assessment of Teachers' MI Strengths

With a few examples, you can easily introduce the concept of MI and give teachers a sense of their own strengths. First make up a set of "Directions to My House" that involve at least five turns through the local neighborhood. Encourage the workshop participants to remember these and then read the directions out loud once. Ask who can repeat them to you (a few will raise their hand, and that's not the important point anyway!). Now ask, "How did each of us remember those directions?" Describe a linguistic/linear memory approach (e.g., "Were you mentally writing out directions, and did you get to a decision point in the journey and begin a new line mentally?"). Some teachers will raise their hands to indicate they did; these are linguistic learners. Then ask, "How many of you were drawing little maps inside your head?" Again, some will raise their hands—they are spatial learners. Finally ask, "How many of you were either moving your hand across the desk to represent that map, or moving your feet quietly under the table for the same reason?" These may be bodily/kinesthetic learners. Indicate that some bodily/kinesthetic learners actually "dance" around the classroom to remember the directions.

2. Use an Informal MI Inventory

There are many informal inventories available on the Internet; using one of these to show that each workshop participant can assess his or her own strengths in MI can be a useful beginning for the workshop. After participants have completed their inventories, score them and discuss the various learning strengths you identify among workshop participants.

3. Planning a Differentiated Instruction Math Unit

Working in small groups, have teachers identify a particular standard or objective within the math curriculum. Using that specific content, have teachers plan a ten-day instructional unit based on this concept, and develop a series of instructional activities that involve all of the multiple intelligences during that unit. Remind them to plan multiple activities for each of the ten days, since on many days classes may do more than one instructional activity. Check to see that all multiple intelligences are involved across the unit, and discuss this planning process with each group of teachers. Finally, have each small group share their instructional ideas with the larger group.

4. Evaluating the Differentiated Math Unit

Conduct the activity in number 3. After the small groups share their ideas with the larger group, conduct a follow-up activity by using the grid provided within the chapter as an evaluation tool. Have each group of teachers identify activities within their ten-day unit that address the concepts at concrete, representational, and abstract levels, using various multiple intelligences. Note that providing a concrete learning example and discussing it with students effectively provides both representational and abstract learning opportunities. However, providing an abstract instructional example followed by discussion does not necessarily address concrete or representational learning needs. Challenge teachers to consider the distinctions between concrete, representational, and abstract learning.

5. Differentiated Instruction/Inclusion Discussion

As a closing discussion on this chapter, you may wish to hold a whole group discussion about the relationship between differentiated instruction and inclusion. Differentiated classes are, almost by definition, general education classes, and there is a nice fit between the concept of differentiated classes, with various groups of students doing various activities, and the inclusive class, which is likely to have more than one teacher in the class.

CHAPTER 2: PLANNING FOR DIFFERENTIATED INSTRUCTION IN MATHEMATICS

Major Points in Chapter 2

In many ways, Chapter 2 is the most important chapter of this text. While there are many effective instructional ideas available in mathematics, the best ideas in the world will not help teachers unless teachers understand fully how to plan an instructional lesson that will allow them to implement those ideas. Without insight into how to effectively plan an instructional lesson that offers differentiated activities to students with different needs, teachers may be left with many effective instructional strategy ideas and no understanding as to how those ideas may be used. The core of this chapter involves the juxtaposition of a direct instruction lesson plan and the modifications of that direct instruction plan that will result in a highly differentiated lesson.

Chapter 2 begins with a description of the lesson-planning process that has become second nature to teachers today—the direct instructional lesson-planning process. This includes orientation to the daily lesson, teacher led instruction, teacher guided practice, independent practice, and assessment as reteaching. In contrast, the differentiated instructional lesson suggests that after each of the phases above, the teacher should use the Guess, Assess, and Tear Out Tactic to identify a subgroup of students for a differentiated activity.

The results of the Guess, Assess, and Tear Out technique should be discussed at length. These are presented in one of the chapter's highlighted boxes. Because this technique results in various groups of students doing different tasks in the math class, one concern is about the management of these students. Discuss with the teachers how they may manage the various groups of students after these differentiated math groups are formed. Point out that many teachers currently use various instructional subgroups within the class; discuss how this is similar to the differentiated lesson plan presented here.

General Discussion Questions

1. Begin the lesson with a discussion of the universal application of direct instructional lesson planning in math. You may wish to have teachers bring in their math curricula and identify within those teacher's manuals the various aspects of the direct instructional lesson plan.

2. After discussing direct instruction in math, challenge the teachers to consider the question, "Who really needed this lesson delivered in this way?" For example, are some of the higher ability students in the general education classroom already competent in this area of math? In short, do those students need

to be taught this lesson? Further, if we know, after the orientation to the lesson, that some kids literally know the material and don't need that lesson, is it appropriate to continue to teach that lesson to them? Will they be bored, and are they likely to misbehave?

3. In contrast, are other students in the class likely to have significant challenges with this lesson? Do those students need more prerequisite instruction for that lesson, and thus more teacher time? How can we vary the direct instructional lesson discussed above in order to differentiate the math class and provide these students with the learning activities they truly need?

4. Can the Guess, Assess, and Tear Out Tactic work in the typical general education math class with some 20 to 30 students? What is likely to happen when several groups of students are working relatively independently of teacher supervision? Do behavior problems arise? How can they be managed?

5. Have educators nationally prepared students to work in cooperative groups on educational tasks in math, without direct supervision of the teacher? Should the ability to work in such a fashion be one goal of education?

6. Point out that the first two chapters of this text provide different thoughts on lesson planning. Whereas the lesson-planning grid in the first chapter addressed the application of multiple intelligence activities across an instructional unit in math, Chapter 2 focuses on one specific daily lesson in math. Differentiated math classes will employ both of these planning mechanisms in order to offer effective, differentiated math lessons for all students in the class. You may wish to ask teachers, "Which of these instructional planning mechanisms do you believe you will find more effective?"

7. Discuss the relationship between the National Council of Teachers of Mathematics (NCTM) standards in math, and the application of differentiated instruction. Do the standards allow appropriate flexibility to develop and plan differentiated math lessons that result in high levels of involvement of students? When differentiated lessons are offered, and children are more involved in their learning activities, what is likely to be the result of that increased involvement on their overall achievement?

Workshop Activity Ideas

1. The Guess, Assess, and Tear Out Activity

The core of this chapter is the lesson planning activity, Guess, Assess, and Tear Out. As a major focus of the workshop, this idea should be discussed at length. Next, a walk-through of this type of instructional lesson should be conducted. The discussion questions above can be used to lead this activity. Break the workshop participants into small groups, and assign each of the questions above as a discussion topic for one of the groups. Give the groups 15 minutes to formulate an answer to their question, and then share those thoughts with the whole group.

2. Finding Tear Out Ideas

One question I typically ask about the Guess, Assess, and Tear Out Tactic is, "Where do we find these interesting and innovative math instructional ideas?" Rather than share the ideas in the text (i.e., that teachers do not have to generate these ideas—they are printed in the teacher's manuals where they are referred to as "enrichment ideas" or "additional teaching suggestions"), hold a whole group discussion concerning where these additional ideas for the differentiated groups may come from. Base the discussion on the teacher's manuals for the curriculum the teachers are using currently, and then have teachers, working in grade level groups, review some of those activities and consider their application as tear out activities.

3. Who Gets What Instruction?

One interesting discussion topic involves the differences between the instruction offered to the tear out groups compared to instruction offered to the mainline group. After teachers have practiced differentiated instruction in math for a while, what differences, if any, would they expect to see between the instruction offered to tear out groups and groups in the main line of instruction? Make sure the discussion group considers the questions presented in the text concerning Ms. Adrian's instruction for the mainline group in her class.

4. Relating Instruction to State Standards in Math

After the discussion above concerning differences between instruction offered to tear out groups compared to instruction offered to students in the mainline group, consider the implications this may hold for assessment at the end of the math unit. Are different assessments in order for children receiving instruction in different ways? What implication does this hold for state mandated assessments? Point out that almost all nationally available math curricula relate the lessons to either standards for a particular state or the NCTM standards.

Applicability of Tear Out Groups

After discussion of this tear out idea and its implications, teachers can be challenged by the overall question, "Can this work in your math class?" For teachers who indicate this probably wouldn't work, inquire if there are particular problems that they can see in advance. In some cases, those problems may result from the disruptive behavior of one or two students. If that is the case, perhaps the idea would be workable if that general education teacher could receive the support of the special education teachers for that math period.

CHAPTER 3: DIFFERENTIATING FOR ABSTRACT MATH COMPREHENSION

Major Points in Chapter 3

Chapter 3 offers a bridge from the number sense level of pre-math skills to the understanding of early operations. For workshop purposes, I often find that

I do "less theory and more practical," and as a result I do not tend to emphasize the UDSSI model or the early math model presented herein in most workshops. It may be helpful, however, to review the levels of learning early mathematics presented in the early section of the chapter.

The chapter offers an array of instructional strategies that are proven by research. The concept of three-tiered learning—concrete, semi-concrete, abstract, or the CSA model—is described at length. Point out that this concept has been around for a long time, and while many teachers have used this idea in early math, what brain research and differentiated instructional emphasis suggests is increased use of this CSA concept in higher grade levels. While reviews of research are not heavily emphasized in this book, the brief description of the application of CSA in a fourth-grade classroom should be discussed. Note that all students in that inclusive fourth-grade classroom improved their performance based on CSA instruction—including not only students with disabilities or math deficits, but also normally functioning kids and even gifted kids. After reviewing that study with the group, a discussion of the various pictures that can assist higher grade teachers with three-digit numbers would be appropriate. This is how semi-concrete or representational learning can be moved upward in the grades. Along those lines, you should also briefly point out the CSA example of the algebraic equation presented in the chapter.

The several errorless learning procedures presented here offer students in lower grade levels the opportunity to experience math without experiencing failure in math. As shown in Chapter 1, many students associate mathematics with a negative emotional reaction, and negative emotional impact prohibits effective learning. For this reason, every teacher moving into differentiated instruction in math should have several errorless learning tactics available for particular students. In particular, the time delay tactic can be of great benefit for math facts across the elementary grades.

Finally, the classwide peer tutoring tactic presented here offers one of the most effective ways to provide highly differentiated lessons, since each person is receiving tutored instruction exactly on his or her level. This tactic should be stressed as a teaching tool that should be utilized in virtually every math class.

General Discussion Questions

1. At the beginning of any workshop, a discussion of the CSA tactic is a good idea. Of course, teachers will be aware of this concept but may not have heard of the reemphasis it has received across the grade levels. A review of the research articles described in the chapter is an excellent idea; also, emphasize that all students—including gifted students—benefited from this approach. Also, review the algebraic example for the workshop participants, because that example demonstrates the applicability of this approach throughout the elementary grades. In order to relate this CSA tactic to the multiple intelligences concept, ask teachers, "Which intelligences are addressed in CSA instruction?"

2. Errorless learning procedures should be discussed as the answer to the age-old question, "What do I do with nonmotivated kids who hate math?"

Because early math learning is associated with failure for so many kids, many students develop negative emotional baggage concerning their own math achievement. To counteract this, teachers should have a variety of errorless learning activities that can be used in any math area in the elementary grades.

3. Discuss the example in the text of Mr. Varella's use of the time delay tactic. Print out and share in the workshop the time delay recording sheet and have several workshop participants describe its use. This tactic should be one's instructional strategy of choice for students who have difficulty in such tasks as memorizing math facts tables and the like. Ask the workshop participants if any of them have used any of these errorless learning procedures previously. As a follow-up question, ask if the teachers can identify any students with particular strengths or weaknesses in particular aspects of the multiple intelligences for whom this tactic may be inappropriate.

4. Classwide peer tutoring is an instructional innovation that has the effect of involving all students in the learning process more effectively than almost any other learning technique available. To put it simply, all students are involved 100 percent of the time, because all students have a task they must perform 100 percent of the time. Because of the importance of this technique, spend some time describing its usefulness as an "instructional practice" technique. When tear out groups are doing movement-based activities and other exciting stuff, the classwide peer tutoring tactic can be used in mainline instruction to make it every bit as interesting and exciting.

5. Coupling several teaching ideas together can make for an interesting discussion for either small or large groups. Discuss how the errorless learning procedures described earlier may be coupled with another technique in this chapter—classwide peer tutoring—to offer errorless learning to all students in the elementary class at the same time.

Workshop Activity Ideas

1. A Representational Example Search Activity

If your workshop participants range across the grade levels, have a variety of those teachers at different grade levels bring in their math teachers manuals and compare the number of representational examples across the grade levels. Have three teachers in Grade 1, standing together, find four examples of representational problems. After those four examples are found, have those teachers raise their hands. Beginning at the same time, have the teachers in Grade 3, standing to one side of the Grade 1 teachers, search their instructors manuals for four representational problems, and raise their hands once they find them. Finally, have a group of Grade 5 or Grade 6 teachers search and indicate when they have located four representational examples. This activity will show that while representational examples are typically available across the grade levels in the current curricula, there are many more examples in lower grade materials. Of course, the emphasis here is that teachers in Grades 5 and 6 should be using representational examples just as much as teachers in Grades 1 or 2.

2. Ideas for Using CSA in Higher Math

Have three groups of three teachers each assist in this activity. Each group should be provided with a piece of chart paper and a bold marker. They will work in front of the workshop group. Provide each of these teams with several algebraic equations, and challenge them to find a way to graphically represent these for students in the class. To get other workshop participants involved, allow the remaining workshop participants to "shout an idea" to their friends and colleagues at the charts in the front of the room. After five minutes or so, have the teams share their ideas with the larger audience, and point out how creative teachers can, in fairly short order, generate representational ideas for higher level math.

3. Review the "Ideas From Teachers"

Appoint a small group to discuss the several teaching ideas presented in the "Ideas From Teachers" sections in this chapter. Describe how these ideas exemplify both CSA instruction and the application of instruction in multiple intelligences. Are there additional ideas that participants in the workshop can share? If so, have various participants write their CSA tactics on a piece of chart paper, and the whole group should discuss each of these. Sharing ideas in this way can be one of the most effective workshop techniques available, and having teachers leave the workshop with an array of classroom tested ideas is a wonderful motivator for teachers.

4. Role-Play for Time Delay Learning

Develop a role-play activity that demonstrates an errorless learning procedure. Using the descriptions of the procedure in the chapter, have one workshop participant, acting as the teacher, present the seven times tables to another participate (i.e., the "student"). Instruct the teacher to present the ten facts in that multiplication table using a zero-second delay and counting correct responses from the student. Next, have the math facts presented using a three-second delay. Prior to beginning, rehearse the "student" on getting some of these wrong in order to demonstrate scoring for the incorrect anticipations, and so on. After this activity, debrief the participants in terms of how they felt during the learning process.

5. Role-Play Classwide Peer Tutoring

The classwide peer tutoring tactic described here may be the most important differentiated instructional tactic, since this mode of instruction offers the teacher a way to involve all students in the learning process at the same time, even with 25 or 30 students in the math class. Workshop providers may wish to develop a role-play activity that demonstrates how two students working on different division facts tables can be used to tutor each other for a time. Rather than ten-minute tutoring sessions, as recommended for the classroom, the workshop may demonstrate three-minute tutoring sessions. After the demonstration is completed, ask the teachers who participated in the role play to describe the possible use of this technique. Also, speculate on what the "emotional" results might be for some students who are used to failure in math.

CHAPTER 4: DIFFERENTIATING FOR CONCEPTUAL DEVELOPMENT AND DEEP UNDERSTANDING

Major Points in Chapter 4

Chapter 4 challenges teachers to directly address the toughest of all instructional problems in the differentiated math class—development of deep conceptual understandings of various mathematics principles. Of course, the clear direction of the NCTM standards is toward deep conceptual understanding, and many believe that the constructivist concept that is the foundation for this chapter offers the best approach to this challenge. Tactics such as cognitively guided inquiry and scaffolding are frequently presented in the research and practitioner's literature as effective mathematics instructional tactics. Yet while some see distinctions between these tactics, other teachers see these as various faces of the same general constructivist idea.

Whereas behavioral thought (which was the basis for much of Chapter 3) and metacognitive thought (which is the basis for much of the next chapter) have been around for a long while, constructivist thought is much more recent. As a result, while I am always careful in considering how much time to devote to "theory" in a workshop, I typically do spend a bit of time on constructivist theory as a backdrop for subsequent work. The example of cognitively guided inquiry provides an excellent example of how a teacher can assist a student in constructing new knowledge.

The concept of scaffolded instruction is directly tied to constructivist thinking. In fact, many would argue that cognitively guided inquiry and scaffolding are synonymous. For those teachers, scaffolding will by definition involve a teacher in determining a student's exact level of understanding of a math concept and then providing supports for moving that student to the next level of learning. Further, the teacher is the essential element since he or she must decide exactly when to withdraw the supports offered to the student in order to assure independence in learning. This is the more traditional definition of scaffolded instruction.

Others, however, see scaffolding as a broader concept. For these teachers, scaffolding supports may be either a teacher using guided questions or a chart of steps to complete while attempting a certain type of math problem. For these teachers, supports may be anything that is directly tied to the student's current level of understanding. It is quite likely that the workshop will include persons who have these varied understandings of scaffolding, and you may wish to consider this as an interesting discussion item. The word problem map may serve as one example of a scaffold that is usable for a variety of students. You may wish to discuss how this map may be adapted to higher grade levels or for particular types of problems.

Depending on the workshop participants, other tactics described in this chapter may serve as the basis for extended discussion. For example, if teachers are using a curriculum that emphasizes partial products, the modifications described herein may serve as appropriate discussion topics. Certainly, the process mnemonics example provided should be reviewed at some length. Point out that for some students, the likeness between this process mnemonics example (i.e., subtraction as "defenders" and "attackers") and the combative basis of many modern video games makes this teaching tactic a strategy that all teachers should utilize for some kids.

General Discussion Questions

1. The constructivist perspective should be discussed at length, as it serves as the basis for many of the concepts presented here. One focus of the discussion may be a question such as, "What distinctions do you see between the concepts and tactics described in this chapter?" Some teachers may argue that cognitively guided inquiry is merely one form of scaffolding, and that each is an example of constructivist thinking. However, other teachers may see distinctions between these ideas.

2. After a discussion of constructivist thought, you may wish to briefly review the NCTM standards while making the point that, of all the major instructional approaches, the constructivist approach probably represents the "best fit" with those standards. Both emphasize deep understandings rather than rote performance, and each involves activating student thinking.

3. Review and discuss the cognitively guided inquiry dialogue presented at length in the chapter. This example can be used as a basis for a discussion of what types of questions teachers may ask, or what the indicators are that more suggestive questions may be necessary. Also, inquire of teachers about the types of students who may learn very effectively in this arrangement. For example, would students with a poorly developed interpersonal intelligence learn well in this type of instructional arrangement?

4. Discuss the differences, if any, between cognitively guided inquiry and scaffolding. While some may perceive these as different techniques, others may not.

5. While many math curricula explicitly teach the recognition of cue words in math problems, not all curricula present the same words or emphasize them to the same degree. Invite the teachers to discuss use of cue words in math problems with questions like, "Do you emphasize the search for cue words to your students?" "Is it more problematic to determine the meanings of various cue words in certain types of problems?"

6. The concept of schema-based instruction is presented here, as the basis for graphic representations of word problems. While this concept involves the eventual expectation that students will develop their own graphic representations for various word problem schemas, the focus in lower grade graphic representation is on having the student employ graphics that the teacher has developed, and merely enter the information from the word problem into the graphic. Some students, however, may be ready for the higher level use of story schemas (as presented in the next chapter). You may wish to emphasize the

diversity of cognitive levels by asking teachers, "Can you identify students in your class who would need the support of a graphic device, as well as others who should be required to develop their own?" How does the use of graphic devices relate to the concept of multiple intelligences?

7. Many teachers are used to using various forms of graphic representations in math instruction, and for students who learn in spatial ways, graphic representations can be critical. Questions that can be used to initiate this discussion include, "Who can share an unusual way to use a graphic representation in a math class?" "How did that teaching tactic work for you?" Asking broad questions like these offers participants in the workshop the opportunity to share tactics that they may already be using, and many teachers find such a sharing of ideas helpful.

8. The modification tactics described in this chapter should be reviewed with the workshop participants. While these ideas are not new, they do provide a basis for both tear out and mainline instruction, and they can be relatively easy to teach. In particular, the expanded notation concept works well for students who have strengths in both spatial and naturalistic learning.

9. Discuss at length the process mnemonics suggestions from the highlighted text in the chapter. It is often interesting to note how making whole number and decimal number operations into a game can excite and motivate various students. This activity is very appropriate for either a tear out activity or a mainline instructional activity.

Workshop Activity Ideas

1. A Search for Constructivist Thinking in the Math Curriculum

Using several teachers manuals of various grade levels from the curriculum used in the local school district, have several small groups of teachers work together and search for examples of scaffolded instruction, cognitively guided inquiry, or process mnemonics that may be available in the local school curriculum. If few examples are found, you should stress the innovative nature of these approaches. If several examples are available (and they will be for mnemonics, if not specifically for scaffolded instruction or guided inquiry), point out how these approaches are already being used in mathematics. Teachers typically respond quite favorably to seeing how innovative ideas are embedded within their current curriculum.

2. Develop a Graphic Representation

This activity has three phases. First, form teachers into small groups of four or five; you may present a math problem to four such groups, and present a different math problem to another four groups. Challenge each group to develop a graphic representation of their problem and allow them ten minutes to note their ideas on large chart paper. Next, the second phase involves having the groups who were working on the same problem meet to compare their graphic ideas. This may take 15 minutes or so. Finally, phase three involves having the whole group meet together so that every participant hears a variety of graphic representation ideas dealing with several different math problems.

3. A Cooperative Teaching Exercise for the Workshop

Use the mnemonics suggestions for whole number and decimal operations as the basis for a "cooperative learning jigsaw tactic" in your workshop. Divide the participants into teams of four persons. Give the first person in each team only the information on subtraction, the second person the information on addition, the third the information on multiplication, and the fourth the information on division. Initially, use the "expert team member" concept in which all "number one team members" (i.e., those specializing in subtraction) meet and discuss ways to teach that form of subtraction to their team members. At the same time, other team members are also meeting in expert teams and discussing addition, multiplication, and division. Next, have the original teams reform and share tactics so that each teacher learns how to use this process mnemonics concept to teach the operations with whole and decimal numbers.

4. A Focused Discussion of Scaffolding

While some of the participants may have used scaffolding previously, many have not done so. In my workshops, I sometimes ask if any teachers have used a particular strategy, such as scaffolding, and if some indicate they have, ask them if they would be comfortable explaining their application of scaffolding to the other workshop participants. Further, you may wish to "lead" this discussion toward the broader ideas of constructivist learning.

CHAPTER 5: DIFFERENTIATING FOR ELEMENTARY WORD PROBLEM SOLVING

Major Points in Chapter 5

Perhaps no instructional approach or theory of learning has impacted mathematics instruction as much as the metacognitive instructional approach described in Chapter 5. Although metacognitive thought has been one of the dominant theories in education and mathematics instructional pedagogy for more than two decades, some teachers may not have a strong background in this perspective. For example, some teachers believe that merely putting a poster of a particular learning strategy acronym on the wall constitutes metacognitive instruction, and while those persons are fairly rare, there is a common misconception about the time commitment required to do effective metacognitive instruction in the classroom. In short, effective metacognitive instruction takes time—and in many cases, more time than teachers allow. The overall research, however, is strongly supportive of using metacognitive approaches for instruction in word problems.

Initially in this chapter several metacognitive approaches are described, including RIDD, the STAR strategy, and the SQRQCQ tactic. While there are a variety of differences between these tactics, the workshop facilitator can compare them with each other and highlight the bases of metacognitive instruction.

Independent of the various learning strategy acronyms themselves, the methods used to teach students the various learning strategies are the same. The instructional guidelines presented in the highlighted boxes in the chapter should be emphasized, as these are the basis for all learning-strategy instruction. Also, you should point out that learning strategy instruction represents a long-term investment over a period of days or weeks, but the benefits of this instruction remain with the students their entire lifetime.

The schema-based instructional idea presented herein is an extension of the graphic representation idea from Chapter 4. The emphasis in this chapter, however, is on a higher order involvement with the concept, in that students should be trained to recognize the different schema involved in word problems. Much like training on recognition of cue words, teaching students to recognize the different schema in word problems will take a period of days, but this instructional tactic is very effective as a tear out tactic for students who need a higher level challenge in the mathematics curriculum. Those students, in turn, may be used to teach others to recognize word problem schema in subsequent activities.

General Discussion Questions

1. You should begin by discussing the steps involved in the solution of a simple addition or subtraction problem involving regrouping. You should refer to the simple whole number addition problem described in the first part of the chapter, and the list of separate steps necessary in order to complete that problem successfully. Point out that even simple problems involve a series of sequenced steps, and that many students with difficulties in math have problems with sequenced tasks such as this.

2. Discuss the guidelines used to teach learning strategies. Emphasize that instruction in any learning strategy involves much more than merely making the acronym available to students. Teachers should give students repeated practice in recognition of when to use or not use a particular strategy. Once students have begun to use learning strategies, they will typically see the benefits of these tactics. You may wish to ask the workshop participants, "How many of you have done extended instruction in learning strategies with your students?" Some participants probably have, while others have merely introduced the concept. Phrasing the question as suggested here should encourage those who have used this approach extensively to participate in the discussion.

3. Discuss the comparative application of the first three strategies presented in this chapter. What types of things are encouraged in these strategies? In what ways are these strategies similar or different? What are the strengths and weaknesses of each strategy? To get the discussion going, point out that the RIDD and STAR strategies are similar in that both emphasize making a drawing of the problem, but that the STAR strategy explicitly tells the student to read the problem a second time, whereas the RIDD strategy does not. Is that difference more or less important for certain students?

4. Discuss with the participants the use of nonsense words to represent terms in the math problem that the student does not understand, as suggested by the RIDD tactic. Can this be an effective tactic? Are there students whose reading and comprehension of the word problem is inhibited by one unknown word? Have any of the participants seen this problem among students in their class? How do students with a strength in linguistic learning do with this tactic, compared to students with strengths in other multiple intelligences?

5. In some ways, the STAR strategy is the essence of math word problems. While this strategy, like RIDD, uses visualization, this tactic emphasizes translating the word problem into a meaningful mathematical equation. Discuss this emphasis with the participants.

6. Schema-based instruction has received a great deal of research attention. For some children—in particular, learners with a strength in logical/mathematical thinking or naturalistic learners who need to understand the "whole to part" sense of word problems—teaching the word problem story schema tactic can be particularly effective. Ask if any participants have used this approach to word problems before (it is not likely that many teachers have, since this is very recent). Next, spend 15 minutes or so reviewing the various simple story schemas and another 15 minutes on word problems that involve multiple story schemas. Challenge teachers to use this story schema approach as an interesting tear out activity for students who have difficulty understanding the broad questions in the math word problem.

Workshop Activity Ideas

1. Walking Through Metacognition

Ask the participants to give you a sample whole number math problem. Have an "assistant" come to the front and write it on chart paper. The sample problem may involve any operation. Ask the assistant to work the problem and, with your help, voice his or her steps in the thinking process, and have another "assistant" write those steps on another chart at the front of the room. The list should roughly parallel the list found in the text in the early part of the chapter. At the end of the problem, call attention to the number of separate steps that must be done in sequence in order to get the correct answer to the problem. Ask the audience, "How well can your students with difficulties in math do this type of sequenced activity?" Then explain that metacognitive instruction focuses directly on strengthening that type of step-by-step understanding.

2. An Activity on Teaching Learning Strategies

Pick one of the learning strategies presented in this chapter and walk through the teaching process for that strategy. Learning-strategy training usually involves practice with the same learning strategy over a period of a few weeks. First, students must be fluent in the steps in the strategy. They need to see and explore multiple examples of how to apply the strategy, and then strategy usage should be constantly referred to in their mathematics curriculum. In workshops I typically teach one of the learning strategies, and then merely describe the others. I usually allow approximately 20 minutes for this activity.

3. The Learning Strategies Expert Panel

As an alternative, if you have some teachers who have used the learning strategies approach extensively, you may form an "expert panel" by seating these persons at the front of the workshop and, using leading questions, have them describe their instructional experience using this approach.

4. Debate the Strategies

Learning strategies instruction is quite extensive and goes far beyond merely instruction in math. In fact, it seems each time one picks up a journal another instructional strategy is presented for teaching math word problems to students. Have the participants nominate three-member "debate teams" without knowing what the debate task will be. After teams are formed, assign one learning strategy (RIDD, STAR, or SQRQCQ) to each team. Have the debate teams prepare for five to ten minutes by listing "talking points" that favor the use of one particular strategy. Then hold a *"Debate on the Strategies"* for the whole group for about 20 minutes, with each team arguing for application of their strategy rather than the others. To conclude the debate, thank the teams with a round of applause and then point out the various strengths and weaknesses of the tactics that came to light in the debate.

CHAPTER 6: DIFFERENTIATING FOR HIGHER ORDER LEARNING

Major Points in Chapter 6

While many of the instructional suggestions included previously are appropriate across the elementary grade levels, Chapter 6 focuses on several suggestions for higher level mathematics. First, the anchored instruction concept has received a great deal of research attention, and results have shown this tactic to be effective. Use of video examples of real-world math problems can result in motivating the unmotivated students in the differentiated class, and the effect of anchored instruction on students with disabilities in the math class is no less than phenomenal. Further, the opportunity to enhance anchored instruction can add credibility to learning, even beyond the real-world video examples. Having students do practical projects based in anchored math is certainly an effective instructional technique. The curricula that are currently available for instruction using anchored instruction are limited, however. Mention to the teachers in the workshop that their math curriculum materials will soon include various video anchors as a matter of course, and that this instructional procedure is, most assuredly, in their near future.

Next, the PASS theory represents both a theory of intelligence as well as an effective instructional strategy that can assist more mature learners of mathematics to concentrate on their own effective learning skills. The letters in PASS stand for specific mental functions that are the basis of much of the conceptual learning in mathematics as follows.

P *Planning* to do the math problem

A *Attention* to the details in the problem

S *Simultaneous* consideration of various aspects of the problem

S *Successive* attention to the sequencing of partial answers necessary to solve the problem

As discussed in Chapter 1, one foundation of differentiated instruction is the emphasis on teaching students to consider the academic content in terms of their own learning strengths, as represented by multiple intelligences. In PASS theory, each of the factors above is viewed as a separate "mental function." By teaching these various mental functions with PASS as necessary components of problem solving, students can learn the importance of these functions in their math assignments. Thus, PASS fits nicely into the overall differentiated instructional approach. Students should learn not only the steps in task solution, but also how those steps may be specifically targeted by their own mental processes.

Further, because of the daily requirement of "ten minutes to reflectively consider this type of math problem" embedded in the PASS approach, students become quite efficient at considering their own mental processes while they complete math problems. Further, this group reflective discussion offers one way to strengthen the interpersonal intelligence of students, since this represents a daily interpersonal activity in the math class.

The chapter closes with eight principles for teachers to keep in mind concerning the design of mathematics activities of higher level learners in the upper grades. These principles represent an accumulation of thought from a variety of areas. Teachers may "see" within these guidelines points that have been made previously in association with one instructional tactic or another. The purpose of presenting these here is to prepare students for a successful transition into secondary school with its much more demanding mathematics requirements.

General Discussion Questions

1. As an introductory activity for the participants, you may wish to discuss the applicability of some of the strategies and tactics discussed previously. You may ask, "Which of the strategies described in Chapters One through Five of this book would be applicable in Grade Eight?" The purpose of this discussion would be to drive home the point that almost all of the strategies presented in this text are very appropriate across all the grade levels, either as tear out tactics or mainline instructional ideas. While one should not spend a great deal of workshop time on this point, it is probably worth a five-minute discussion.

2. While anchored instruction has not yet impacted the currently available mathematics curricula, there is every reason to believe that it soon will. Point out that this type of learning can motivate the unmotivated student, and that math publishers are quickly realizing how inexpensive it is to develop video anchors for math problems. Ask if any teachers have used this approach yet (it is likely that only a few, if any, have). Follow that point up with the question, "How long do you think it will be before such video anchors are provided when we adopt a new math curriculum?"

3. Discuss PASS theory, emphasizing the dual nature of this approach. This is both a theory of intelligence as well as a learning strategy. Describe at length the PASS lesson, as presented in the text, focusing on the ten-minute dialogue portion of the lesson.

4. Many teachers will have some difficulty with the suggestion that the teacher not lead the ten-minute discussion of the math problems. These authors, however, as reported in the text, feel that it is critical that students make a decision to discuss the math problems on display, and that even if they choose to talk about other things for a day or so, that should be allowed. Ask your participants about their thoughts on this aspect of the PASS approach.

5. Depending on the grade level of the teachers in the workshop, a discussion of the eight principles for designing math activities for higher level learners may be held. Point out that even in classes where many learners are not succeeding in math, the differentiated math class will require tear out instructional ideas for many advanced or gifted students. These suggestions may help in addressing that need.

Workshop Activity Ideas

1. Demonstrate an Anchored Instruction Video Math Problem

Several anchored instruction curricula are currently available on the market, and if one of these is available to you, you should consider showing one or two problems from that video to the group. Describe the likely effect of the use of such "concrete" problems on the learning curve for students in an elementary math class.

2. A Discussion of a Talking Points Activity

After discussion of the PASS strategy and a critical review of the early and later probe questions, you should break the participants up into small groups of six participants or so. In each group, one participant should play the role of the teacher and the others should play the role of students engaged in a ten-minute debriefing of a page of math problems. Present each group with an example of a long division problem with a two-digit divisor and a remainder. Next, have each group write a "dialogue" of the ten-minute teacher and student discussion of the student's solution to the math problem. Assign some groups to generate a dialogue based on the early probe questions in the chapter and some groups to use the later probe questions. Present these dialogues to the whole group for discussion.

3. Principles for Designing Higher Order Math Activities

Eight principles are presented for designing higher order math activities in the upper grades. Break the audience into eight subgroups, and have each group discuss one of these principles for 15 minutes. Participants should feel free to challenge the principle, to agree or disagree with it, or to add to it. The thoughts from each group should be presented to the whole group as a culminating activity.